The Ultimate History Quiz

B.R. Egginton

Contents

Preface

'A people without knowledge of their past, origin and culture is like a tree without roots,' Marcus Garvey said many years ago.

Yet, like most lessons history can teach us, it still rings true today.

Some of the most perplexing mysteries and thrilling adventures ever known happened not in fiction, but in real life. Were the Princes in the Tower really done away with by their uncle? What happened to the crew of the *Mary Celeste*? Was Jack the Ripper a real person? Does the Shroud of Turin bear the image of Jesus Christ?

And in addition to this, the human race's severe lack of ability (or will) to learn from past mistakes is the principal cause of the world's ample problems today: inequality, overpopulation, conflict, famine, tyranny… the answer to all these problems is written down somewhere. All we have to do is look hard enough.

This book explores a broad range of historical periods. From the Pre-Columbian Americas to the Second World War to English monarchs: whatever your interests, you'll find plenty of questions to keep yourself occupied.

Each category is divided into three levels of difficulty: easy (with multiple choice), average and expert.

So whether you're new to the study of history or consider yourself a history buff, this is the quiz book for you.

All that's left to say is prepare to be baffled, awestruck and at times downright frustrated.

For only through struggle can there be progress.

General History

<u>**General History 1 (easy)**</u>

Q1 How was Louis XVI of France executed in 1793?

    A Hung, drawn and quartered
    B Starved
    C Guillotined
    D Firing squad

Q2 The Reconquista refers to the Christian reconquering of which peninsular?

    A Arabian
    B Iberian
    C Balkan
    D Crimean

Q3 The Silk Road connected which continents?

    A Asia, Africa and Europe
    B Africa and Europe
    C North and South America
    D Africa and Asia

Q4 Attila was the ruler of which group?

    A Saxons
    B Jutes
    C Picts
    D Huns

Q5 Reinhard Heydrich was assassinated in which city in 1942?

    A Bratislava
    B Berlin
    C Paris
    D Prague

Q6 What was the world's first underground railway?

    A New York City Subway
    B Paris Metro
    C Moscow Metro
    D London Underground

Q7 Which sociologist is well-known for the concept of a 'Protestant work ethic'?

    A Max Weber
    B Karl Marx
    C Friedrich Engels
    D Emile Durkheim

Q8 In which city was Tsar Alexander II of Russia assassinated?

    A Vladivostok
    B Sarajevo
    C Saint Petersburg
    D Moscow

Q9 How many Boer Wars were there?

    A 1
    B 2
    C 3
    D 4

Q10 Sam Houston was the first president of which country?

    A United States of America
    B South Africa
    C Republic of Texas
    D Haiti

Q1 The poet Lord Byron died in which country?

    A Turkey
    B Greece
    C Macedonia
    D England

Q2 Where were French monarchs crowned?

    A Reims Cathedral
    B Notre-Dame Cathedral
    C Chartres Cathedral
    D Amiens Cathedral

Q3 Which three political leaders attended the Yalta Conference?

    A Clement Attlee, Joseph Stalin and Franklin Roosevelt
    B Winston Churchill, Joseph Stalin and Harry Truman
    C Winston Churchill, Joseph Stalin and Franklin Roosevelt
    D Clement Atlee, Joseph Stalin and Harry Truman

Q4 Who commissioned the Arc de Triomphe?

    A Napoleon I
    B Napoleon III
    C Louis XIV
    D Louis XVI

Q5 What was a Bretwalda in Anglo-Saxon England?

    A Horse
    B Ruler
    C Bishop
    D Weapon

Q6 Eliot Ness was a prohibition agent, famous for his work in which city?

   A Atlanta
   B Chicago
   C Los Angeles
   D New York

Q7 Peter the Hermit is associated with which of the Crusades?

   A First
   B Second
   C Third
   D Fourth

Q8 Leonardo da Vinci died in which country?

   A Italy
   B Spain
   C The Netherlands
   D France

Q9 Which ruler was determined to acquire 'a place in the sun'?

   A Tsar Nicholas II of Russia
   B Charles I of England
   C Kaiser Wilhelm II of Germany
   D Louis XIV of France

Q10 The Great Trek refers to an eastward migration of Dutch-speaking settlers in which present-day country?

   A Zimbabwe
   B Egypt
   C Morocco
   D South Africa

<u>**General History 3 (easy)**</u>

Q1 Who made the first non-stop flight between North America and Europe in 1927?

    A Charles Lindbergh
    B Amelia Earhart
    C Jimmy Doolittle
    D Louis Blériot

Q2 The Masjid al-Haram mosque is located in which holy city?

    A Rome
    B Mecca
    C Jerusalem
    D Kairouan

Q3 The Falklands War was fought between the United Kingdom and which other country?

    A Spain
    B Brazil
    C Argentina
    D USA

Q4 Which country was the first to recognise Mexico's independence in 1836?

    A France
    B Spain
    C United Kingdom
    D USA

Q5 In which present-day country did the Renaissance begin?

    A France
    B England
    C Germany
    D Italy

Q6 During the 17th century Tortuga was a haven for what?

    A Slaves
    B Revolutionaries
    C Pirates
    D Merchants

Q7 Where did Pocahontas die?

    A Jamestown, Virginia
    B Powhatan Confederacy
    C Gravesend, England
    D Mexico City, New Spain

Q8 What was Ellis Island used for between 1892 and 1954?

    A Immigrant inspection station
    B Nuclear device testing
    C Military training
    D A city park

Q9 Fleet Prison was a notorious prison in which city?

    A London
    B Paris
    C Munich
    D New York

Q10 In 1755 a major earthquake almost destroyed which city?

    A London
    B Paris
    C Lisbon
    D Madrid

<u>**General History 4 (easy)**</u>

Q1 Who assassinated President Abraham Lincoln in 1865?

A Lee Harvey Oswald
B James Earl Ray
C Leon Czolgosz
D Charles Wilkes Booth

Q2 What was King Arthur's religion?

A Islam
B Christianity
C Paganism
D Taoism

Q3 Who discovered the Terracotta Army in 1974?

A Archaeologists
B Grave diggers
C Farmers
D Builders

Q4 Who was the first President of the USA?

A George Washington
B James Buchanan
C Abraham Lincoln
D Ulysses Grant

Q5 Which two continents have never been the site of a major military engagement?

A Africa and Australasia
B Africa and Antarctica
C Australasia and Antarctica
D North America and Australasia

Q6 In which city was Archduke Franz Ferdinand assassinated?

    A Belgrade
    B Sofia
    C Sarajevo
    D Zagreb

Q7 'Will no one rid me of this turbulent priest?' is commonly attributed to which English king?

    A Henry I
    B Henry II
    C Richard III
    D Edward II

Q8 Before relocating, where were the New York Yankees originally based?

    A Baltimore
    B Boston
    C Chicago
    D Los Angeles

Q9 Observing what falling from a tree is said to have inspired Sir Isaac Newton's theory on gravity?

    A Pear
    B Peach
    C Orange
    D Apple

Q10 Where did the Prussian explorer Alexander von Humboldt travel extensively?

    A Africa
    B The Americas
    C Australia
    D China

<u>**General History 5 (easy)**</u>

Q1 Which Greek historian wrote *The Histories*?

    A Polybius
    B Herodotus
    C Xenophon
    D Thucydides

Q2 Vasco da Gama, the first European explorer to reach India by sea, was from which country?

    A Spain
    B Italy
    C Portugal
    D Switzerland

Q3 Which two countries were involved in the Opium Wars?

    A Britain and China
    B Britain and Japan
    C France and China
    D Russia and China

Q4 In which battle was Colonel George Armstrong Custer killed?

    A Sand Creek Massacre
    B Battle of the Little Bighorn
    C First Battle of Bull Run
    D Battle of Tom's Brook

Q5 Captain James Cook was killed on which group of islands?

    A Galapagos Islands
    B Antilles
    C Samoan Islands
    D Hawaiian Islands

Q6 Which French king built the Palace of Versailles?

    A Louis XI
    B Louis XIV
    C Charles VI
    D Francis I

Q7 Which animal played a key role in the formation of the Mongol Empire?

    A Pigs
    B Sheep
    C Cows
    D Horses

Q8 The physician William Harvey is best known for his work on which organ of the human body?

    A Heart
    B Lungs
    C Stomach
    D Intestines

Q9 The Mughal Emperor Aurangzeb was a fanatical supporter of what religion?

    A Christianity
    B Hinduism
    C Taoism
    D Islam

Q10 In what decade of the 20th century did the Mexican Revolution take place?

    A 1910's
    B 1930's
    C 1940's
    D 1960's

<u>**General History 6 (easy)**</u>

Q1 Which architect was in charge of the rebuilding of 52 churches, including St Paul's Cathedral, following the Great Fire of London in 1666?

    A Inigo Jones
    B Charles Barry
    C John Vanbrugh
    D Christopher Wren

Q2 What is the oldest tennis tournament in the world?

    A French Open
    B US Open
    C Australian Open
    D Wimbledon

Q3 Which scandal led to the resignation of President Richard Nixon?

    A Crédit Mobilier Scandal
    B Teapot Dome Scandal
    C Watergate Scandal
    D Whiskey Ring Scandal

Q4 Che Guevara was a revolutionary in which country?

    A Argentina
    B Bolivia
    C Brazil
    D Uruguay

Q5 What country was the philosopher David Hume from?

    A England
    B Scotland
    C Wales
    D Ireland

Q6 The Native American chief Tecumseh died during which war?

    A American Revolutionary War
    B American Civil War
    C Seven Years' War
    D War of 1812

Q7 The hymn *Jerusalem* is the unofficial national anthem of which country?

    A England
    B Israel
    C State of Palestine
    D Malta

Q8 Abbas I was Shah of which country?

    A Iran
    B Afghanistan
    C Pakistan
    D Egypt

Q9 Robert Catesby died at which house?

    A Whitwick Manor
    B Holbeche House
    C Boscobel House
    D Mosely Old Hall

Q10 Where did Japan invade in September 1940?

    A The Philippines
    B French Indochina
    C Hong Kong
    D Australia

Q1 The Berlin Conference of 1884-85 regulated European colonisation and trade in which continent?

    A South America
    B Asia
    C Africa
    D Europe

Q2 In what century did Johannes Gutenberg introduce movable type printing in Europe?

    A 13th
    B 14th
    C 15th
    D 16th

Q3 Gibraltar was ceded to the United Kingdom in 1713 in the aftermath of which war?

    A Thirty Years' War
    B Spanish Civil War
    C War of Spanish Succession
    D Crimean War

Q4 What was the first television network to provide 24 hour news coverage?

    A BBC
    B CNN
    C Fox
    D NBC

Q5 The Time of Troubles was a period in which county's history?

    A England
    B France
    C Japan
    D Russia

Q6 Who famously said 'the chief business of the American people is business'?

    A George Washington
    B Ronald Regan
    C Donald Trump
    D Calvin Coolidge

Q7 The Russian revolutionary Georgi Plekhanov died in which country?

    A Austria
    B England
    C Finland
    D Russia

Q8 Who did the British fight at the Battle of Rorke's Drift?

    A Zulus
    B Maasai
    C Yoruba
    D Xhosa

Q9 The Muscovy Company was based in which country?

    A England
    B Germany
    C Poland
    D Hungary

Q10 How was Maximilian I of Mexico executed?

    A Firing squad
    B Hanging
    C Guillotine
    D Electric chair

General History 8 (easy)

Q1 The historian David Starkey specialises in which English historical period?

    A Edwardian
    B Stuart
    C Tudor
    D Victorian

Q2 Darius the Great ruled which empire?

    A Ottoman
    B Achaemenid
    C Mughal
    D Roman

Q3 Who famously said 'Give me liberty or give me death'?

    A George Washington
    B Thomas Jefferson
    C Patrick Henry
    D Martin Luther King

Q4 Longships are commonly associated with which group?

    A Romans
    B Mongols
    C Vikings
    D Celts

Q5 From which continent does the sport Polo originate?

    A Africa
    B Asia
    C Europe
    D South America

Q6 The Ever Victorious Army was led by European officers, but where were the soldiers from?

A China
B India
C North America
D Morocco

Q7 Who wrote the 1852 novel *Uncle Tom's Cabin*?

A Mark Twain
B Jane Austen
C Harriet Beecher Stowe
D Frances Hodgson Burnett

Q8 The Janissaries were an elite infantry unit in which empire?

A Persian Empire
B Mughal Empire
C Russian Empire
D Ottoman Empire

Q9 Who was the first Prime Minister of Israel?

A Yitzhak Rabin
B Benjamin Netanyahu
C Golda Meir
D David Ben-Gurion

Q10 Founded in 1909, Handley Page Limited were known for manufacturing what?

A Ships
B Cars
C Aircraft
D Trains

<u>**General History 9 (easy)**</u>

Q1 Which dictator published *Mein Kampf* in 1925?

    A Benito Mussolini
    B Joseph Stalin
    C Adolf Hitler
    D Josip Broz Tito

Q2 Who is the author of the *Iliad* and the *Odyssey*?

    A Aristotle
    B Homer
    C Plato
    D Euripides

Q3 Who gave the famous 'I have a dream' speech?

    A Malcolm X
    B Nelson Mandela
    C Martin Luther King Jr.
    D Rosa Parks

Q4 A caravel is a type of what?

    A Horse
    B Sword
    C Fortification
    D Ship

Q5 The slave-turned-rebel Nat Turner was from which US state?

    A Maryland
    B Connecticut
    C Virginia
    D Florida

Q6 The Okhrana was a secret police force in which empire?

    A British Empire
    B Roman Empire
    C Spanish Empire
    D Russian Empire

Q7 In what country did the Argentine politician and army officer Juan Manuel de Rosas seek asylum?

    A Brazil
    B Bolivia
    C USA
    D United Kingdom

Q8 Athenian democracy was developed around which century?

    A 5th century BC
    B 3rd century BC
    C 1st century AD
    D 2nd century AD

Q9 The Batavian Revolution occurred in which present-day country?

    A The Netherlands
    B Switzerland
    C Czech Republic
    D Denmark

Q10 In what year was Japan's first railway opened?

    A 1790
    B 1818
    C 1872
    D 1908

<u>General History 10 (easy)</u>

Q1 The assassination of which nobleman sparked World War One?

    A Prince Albert Victor
    B Archduke Franz Ferdinand
    C Wilhelm, German Crown Prince
    D Archduke Ferdinand Karl of Austria

Q2 Which saint was taken as a slave to Ireland?

    A Saint Augustine
    B Saint Patrick
    C Saint George
    D Saint David

Q3 Condottieri were Italian leaders in which field?

    A Politics
    B Military
    C Art
    D Academia

Q4 Which of the following periods in history occurred first?

    A Renaissance
    B Age of Enlightenment
    C Hellenistic Period
    D Reformation

Q5 The *Mayflower* transported the Pilgrim Fathers from which English port to the New World?

    A Dover
    B Southampton
    C Portsmouth
    D Plymouth

Q6 In southern Africa, Boers refers to the descendants of settlers from which country?

    A England
    B France
    C The Netherlands
    D Germany

Q7 The Mountain Meadows massacre occurred in which present-day US state?

    A Oklahoma
    B Texas
    C Tennessee
    D Utah

Q8 Which US President is well-known for saying: 'Speak softly and carry a big stick; you will go far'?

    A Franklin Roosevelt
    B Theodore Roosevelt
    C Woodrow Wilson
    D Dwight Eisenhower

Q9 The Satsuma Rebellion occurred in what country?

    A China
    B Japan
    C India
    D Pakistan

Q10 What is the oldest independent air force in the world?

    A US Air Force
    B French Air Force
    C Royal Air Force
    D German Air Force

<u>**General History 11 (easy)**</u>

Q1 Which Mormon leader founded Salt Lake City?

A Brigham Young
B Joseph Smith
C John Taylor
D Russell Nelson

Q2 The Belgian revolution of 1830-1831 led to their independence from which country?

A France
B The Netherlands
C Germany
D Switzerland

Q3 The fresco *The Triumph of Death* was painted in which century?

A 13th
B 14th
C 15th
D 16th

Q4 Samuel de Champlain founded which Canadian city?

A Montreal
B Toronto
C Calgary
D Quebec City

Q5 A close stool was an early type of what?

A Bed
B Wardrobe
C Portable toilet
D Light switch

Q6 In which city was Leon Trotsky assassinated?

    A Paris
    B Moscow
    C St Petersburg
    D Mexico City

Q7 Which country won the Battle of Tel El Kebir?

    A Egypt
    B France
    C USA
    D United Kingdom

Q8 The Treaty of Guadalupe Hidalgo ended which war?

    A Mexican-American War
    B Spanish-American War
    C War of 1812
    D Anglo-Spanish War

Q9 During which Winter Olympics did the 'Miracle on Ice' occur?

    A Lake Placid 1980
    B Sarajevo 1984
    C Calgary 1988
    D Albertville 1992

Q10 Who was the first President of Turkey?

    A Mustafa Kemal Atatürk
    B Abdülhalik Renda
    C İsmet İnönü
    D Celâl Bayar

Q1 What was the centre of Roman political power?

    A Parliament
    B Capitol Hill
    C The Forum
    D The General Assembly

Q2 From which country did Algeria gain independence in 1962?

    A United Kingdom
    B Belgium
    C The Netherlands
    D France

Q3 A surprise attack by the Japanese on which naval base led to the US entering World War II?

    A Pearl Harbour
    B Portsmouth Naval Shipyard
    C Norfolk Naval Shipyard
    D Port of Los Angeles

Q4 The Charge of the Light Brigade occurred during which war?

    A Seven Years' War
    B Crimean War
    C First Boer War
    D Falklands War

Q5 Who was the first Holy Roman Emperor?

    A Alfred the Great
    B Charlemagne
    C Julius Caesar
    D Louis I

Q6 Where was Mother Teresa born?

    A Kolkata
    B Rome
    C Skopje
    D New Delhi

Q7 Which explorer is the capital city of North Carolina named after?

    A Sir Walter Raleigh
    B Sir Francis Drake
    C Captain James Cook
    D Henry Hudson

Q8 In which American city did Elvis Presley die?

    A Nashville
    B New York
    C Little Rock
    D Memphis

Q9 Military Intelligence, Section 1 (MI1) was set up during which war?

    A Crimean War
    B World War 1
    C World War 2
    D Cold War

Q10 The Kingdom of Cusco was succeeded by which empire?

    A Aztec Empire
    B Inca Empire
    C Roman Empire
    D Mughal Empire

<u>**General History 13 (easy)**</u>

Q1 Karl Marx died in what city?

    A Paris
    B Munich
    C Berlin
    D London

Q2 What was Constantinople named after?

    A An emperor
    B A saint
    C A church
    D A biblical story

Q3 In which city did Princess Diana die in a car crash in 1997?

    A London
    B Paris
    C York
    D Rotterdam

Q4 Who wrote the *Divine Comedy*?

    A Raphael
    B Giovanni Boccaccio
    C Dante Alighieri
    D Desiderius Erasmus

Q5 Cotton Mather is associated with which of the Thirteen Colonies?

    A Connecticut Colony
    B Massachusetts Bay Colony
    C Province of New York
    D Province of South Carolina

Q6 John Wycliffe led which religious movement?

A Mormonism
B Lollardy
C Puritans
D Jehovah's Witnesses

Q7 Terence V. Powderly was a union leader from which country?

A United Kingdom
B USA
C Germany
D The Netherlands

Q8 Who was the only King of Iceland?

A Leif Erikson
B Christian X of Denmark
C Gustav Vasa
D George V of Great Britain

Q9 In which hall was the Treaty of Versailles signed?

A Hall of Mirrors
B Hall of Kings
C Hall of Versailles
D Hall of the French Republic

Q10 What devastated Tokyo in 1923?

A Tornado
B Air raid
C Earthquake
D Famine

<u>**General History 14 (easy)**</u>

Q1 Which shipping company owned the RMS *Titanic*?

    A Cunard Line
    B P&O
    C White Star Line
    D Shaw, Savill & Albion Line

Q2 Manfred, Baron von Richthofen (the Red Baron) was a pilot during which war?

    A Balkan Wars
    B World War One
    C World War Two
    D Korean War

Q3 Genghis Khan founded which empire?

    A Chinese Empire
    B Mongol Empire
    C Ottoman Empire
    D Khmer Empire

Q4 Martin Luther was a central figure in which reformation?

    A Catholic
    B Protestant
    C Orthodox
    D Methodist

Q5 Benjamin Franklin served as President of which US state?

    A New York
    B New Jersey
    C Massachusetts
    D Pennsylvania

Q6 La Navidad was a settlement established by Christopher Columbus on which island?

    A Jamaica
    B Cuba
    C Hispaniola
    D Bermuda

Q7 The Treaty of Shimonoseki was signed by the Qing dynasty and which empire?

    A Russian Empire
    B British Empire
    C Mongol Empire
    D Empire of Japan

Q8 Which pandemic broke out in 1918?

    A Leprosy
    B Yellow Fever
    C Smallpox
    D Influenza

Q9 As well as the United States Army, which other country's army did Douglas MacArthur serve?

    A China
    B Philippines
    C Australia
    D United Kingdom

Q10 Which supermarket chain opened the first self-service grocery store in 1916?

    A Sainsbury's
    B Piggly Wiggly
    C Wal Mart
    D Morrisons

<u>**General History 15 (easy)**</u>

Q1 Which Norse explorer is said to have discovered North America?

    A Leif Erikson
    B Olaf Tryggvason
    C Erik the Red
    D Harald Hardrada

Q2 The Hassan Tower is all that remains of a what after being hit by an earthquake in 1755?

    A Palace
    B Fortress
    C Town hall
    D Mosque

Q3 Who was the first US President to be impeached?

    A Andrew Jackson
    B Abraham Lincoln
    C Andrew Johnson
    D Grover Cleveland

Q4 The Klondike Gold Rush occurred in which country?

    A USA
    B Canada
    C Russia
    D South Africa

Q5 Angkor Thom was the last capital city of which empire?

    A Akkadian Empire
    B Mughal Empire
    C Khmer Empire
    D Achaemenid Empire

Q6 Joseph McCoy is commonly associated with which breed of cattle?

A Texas Longhorn
B Belgian Blue
C Brangus
D Aberdeen Angus

Q7 Hyperinflation affected which currency between 1921 and 1923?

A Pound Sterling
B US Dollar
C German Papiermark
D Yen

Q8 In what city was Alexei Rykov executed?

A Moscow
B Minsk
C St Petersburg
D Helsinki

Q9 Sukarno was a leader in Indonesia's struggle for independence from which country?

A The Netherlands
B Spain
C Portugal
D United Kingdom

Q10 The Profumo affair involved an affair between Christine Keeler and which British politician?

A Winston Churchill
B Vince Cable
C John Profumo
D Enoch Powell

<u>**General History 16 (easy)**</u>

Q1 What was the nationality of the polar explorer Roald Amundsen?

A Norwegian
B Swedish
C German
D English

Q2 Which French king was called the 'Sun King'?

A Charles VIII
B Henry I
C Louis XIV
D Louis XVI

Q3 The Khmer Empire was a predecessor state to which present-day country?

A Vietnam
B Cambodia
C Thailand
D Singapore

Q4 The Winter War was fought between the Soviet Union and which country?

A Denmark
B Germany
C Finland
D USA

Q5 British forces led by Edmund Allenby occupied which city in 1917?

A Istanbul
B Jerusalem
C Berlin
D St Petersburg

Q6 The Simon Commission arrived in what country in 1928?

    A Indonesia
    B The Philippines
    C India
    D Japan

Q7 What began after Alexander Dubček was elected First Secretary of the Communist Party of Czechoslovakia?

    A German invasion of Czechoslovakia
    B Prague Spring
    C Dissolution of the Soviet Union
    D Dissolution of Czechoslovakia

Q8 Approximately how many Soviet citizens died as a result of the Second World War?

    A 1 million
    B 10 million
    C 26 million
    D 50 million

Q9 Lydia Litvyak is best known as being what during the Second World War?

    A Politician
    B Author
    C Fighter pilot
    D Serial killer

Q10 What name was given to Adolf Hitler's first Eastern Front military headquarters?

    A The Nazi Retreat
    B Munich House
    C Wolf's Lair
    D The Bastion of the Fatherland

Q1 How many United States presidents have been assassinated?

    A 1
    B 3
    C 4
    D 5

Q2 Lorenzo de' Medici was a statesman in which Italian republic?

    A Republic of Florence
    B Republic of Venice
    C Republic of Genoa
    D Parthenopean Republic

Q3 What period followed the American Civil War?

    A Antebellum
    B Reconstruction
    C Great Awakening
    D Prohibition

Q4 Indonesia was a colony of which European power?

    A The Netherlands
    B United Kingdom
    C Spain
    D France

Q5 T. E. Lawrence is better known by what name?

    A The Great Gatsby
    B The Scot King
    C Lawrence of Arabia
    D The Mongolian Monk

Q6 The Hollywood Ten were arrested for their alleged involvement in what?

A The KKK
B Alcohol smuggling
C Communism
D Tax evasion

Q7 The Degenerate Art Exhibition was held in which city in 1937?

A Rome
B Berlin
C Zurich
D Munich

Q8 *Kulaks* were a category of affluent peasants in which empire?

A Mughal Empire
B Empire of Japan
C Russian Empire
D Spanish Empire

Q9 Saad Zaghloul was a nationalist revolutionary from which country?

A Saudi Arabia
B Morocco
C Egypt
D Turkey

Q10 The Final Solution culminated in what?

A The Holocaust
B Dissolution of the Soviet Union
C Creation of the United Nations
D The Sand Creek Massacre

Q1 What was the name of Edward Teach's flagship?

    A *Whydah Gally*
    B *Queen Anne's Revenge*
    C *Black Pearl*
    D *Golden Hind*

Q2 Girolamo Savonarola was part of which Catholic religious order?

    A Benedictine
    B Dominican
    C Franciscan
    D Carmelite

Q3 Abraham Lincoln was the first US President from which political party?

    A Libertarian
    B Green
    C Democratic
    D Republican

Q4 Angkor Wat is a temple complex in which country?

    A Laos
    B Thailand
    C Pakistan
    D Cambodia

Q5 The Generation of '80 refers to the governing elite of which country between 1880 and 1916?

    A Argentina
    B Brazil
    C Mexico
    D Costa Rica

Q6 Grigory Zinoviev was executed during which period of political repression?

    A Spanish Inquisition
    B McCarthy Era
    C The Great Purge
    D The *Estado Novo*

Q7 Which country is Ibn Saud the founder of?

    A Jordan
    B Iran
    C United Arab Emirates
    D Saudi Arabia

Q8 Antonín Novotný ruled which country during the 1950s and 1960s?

    A Bulgaria
    B Yugoslavia
    C Czechoslovakia
    D Hungary

Q9 Aleksandr Solzhenitsyn was a notable critic of which country?

    A Soviet Union
    B USA
    C China
    D Japan

Q10 Joseph McCarthy was a Senator from which US state?

    A Minnesota
    B New York
    C Oklahoma
    D Wisconsin

<u>**General History 19 (easy)**</u>

Q1 Josip Broz Tito was president of which country between 1953 and 1980?

A Yugoslavia
B Hungary
C Romania
D Bulgaria

Q2 John of Gaunt held which title?

A Duke of Cornwall
B Duke of York
C Prince of Wales
D Duke of Lancaster

Q3 In which ocean did Captain Edward Smith die?

A Atlantic
B Arctic
C Indian
D Pacific

Q4 The South Sea Company was granted a monopoly by the British government to trade with which continent?

A North America
B South America
C Africa
D Australasia

Q5 Who was nicknamed 'Prince of the Humanists'?

A Plato
B Vasco da Gama
C Voltaire
D Desiderius Erasmus

Q6 J. P. Morgan was a well-known figure in what sector?

A Fast food
B Automotive industry
C Weapons
D Banking

Q7 In what year did the Philippines gain independence from the USA?

A 1899
B 1918
C 1929
D 1946

Q8 Sergey Kirov is believed to have been assassinated on whose orders?

A Vladimir Lenin
B Tsar Nicholas II
C Joseph Stalin
D Nikita Khrushchev

Q9 How many times was Eugene V. Debs a US presidential candidate?

A 0
B 1
C 3
D 5

Q10 The President of which country committed suicide in 1954?

A USA
B Turkey
C Brazil
D Soviet Union

Q1 What type of plane carried out Operation Chastise using bouncing bombs?

A Hurricane
B Mosquito
C Wellington
D Lancaster

Q2 In which country are the ruins of ancient Carthage?

A Morocco
B Egypt
C Tunisia
D Syria

Q3 At which university did Stephen Hawking begin his higher education?

A Harvard
B Cambridge
C Durham
D Oxford

Q4 Genghis Khan was born in which present-day country?

A China
B Russia
C Mongolia
D India

Q5 Ulrich von Hutten was an outspoken critic of which church?

A Orthodox
B Methodist
C Catholic
D Presbyterian

Q6 In what year was the Kansas–Nebraska Act passed?

A 1790
B 1820
C 1854
D 1900

Q7 Agha was an honorific title in which empire?

A Mughal Empire
B Roman Empire
C Ottoman Empire
D Akkadian Empire

Q8 The Battle of Puebla was fought between France and which other country?

A Spain
B Mexico
C Cuba
D USA

Q9 What was the name of the youth organisation of the Nazi Party?

A Nazi Youth
B German Youth
C Hitler Youth
D Scouts

Q10 The Civilian Conservation Corps was established by the administration of which US President?

A Franklin Roosevelt
B Theodore Roosevelt
C William McKinley
D Herbert Hoover

General History 21 (average)

Q1 The Jack the Ripper killings took place in which London district?

Q2 Who was the first Chancellor of Germany?

Q3 Boudicca was the leader of which British tribe?

Q4 From which European country did Angola obtain independence in 1975?

Q5 Theodora was the wife of which Byzantine Emperor?

Q6 Who founded the Boy Scout movement?

Q7 Whose diary provided a detailed account of the Great Fire of London?

Q8 In which city was Girolamo Savonarola executed?

Q9 Who founded the Ptolemaic Kingdom?

Q10 William Howard Russell, widely regarded as one of the first modern war correspondents, wrote for which newspaper?

Q1 Who was the first monarch of the United Kingdom?

Q2 The showman P.T. Barnum was a native of which US state?

Q3 Which Scottish monarch was convicted of treason and beheaded at Fotheringhay Castle in 1587?

Q4 What were the first names of the Rosenbergs: the couple executed in 1953 for spying for the Soviet Union?

Q5 In which country can the most pyramids be found?

Q6 In what city was Martin Luther King Jr assassinated?

Q7 What was famously burned down during the War of 1812?

Q8 Which charity manages Stonehenge?

Q9 Which Roman famously said 'The die is cast'?

Q10 False Dmitry III claimed to be the youngest son of which Russian ruler?

<u>**General History 23 (average)**</u>

Q1 Which work is historian Edward Gibbon most famous for?

Q2 Which university is the oldest still in operation?

Q3 Who discovered penicillin?

Q4 In what year was Korea divided into North Korea and South Korea?

Q5 Offa's Dyke was constructed on the border between which two kingdoms?

Q6 The Great Schism of 1054 refers to the break of communion between which two churches?

Q7 Caesaropapism refers to combining the power of secular government with what else?

Q8 *The Decameron* is a collection of novellas by which author?

Q9 William FitzOsbern was a councillor of which English King?

Q10 Until 1870 the Papal States were a series of territories on the Italian Peninsula under the direct sovereign rule of who?

<u>**General History 24 (average)**</u>

Q1 Which legendary brothers are said to have led the Angles, Saxons and Jutes in their invasion of Britain in the 5th century?

Q2 The Battle of Edessa was fought between which two empires?

Q3 Plato was a student of which philosopher?

Q4 What is the oldest university in Scotland?

Q5 The Hoover Dam was built during the Great Depression between which two US states?

Q6 The Lombard League was formed to counter attempts by who to assert influence over the Italian peninsula?

Q7 What were the three kinds of plague?

Q8 Charles V (born 1500) ruled which two empires?

Q9 Christopher Columbus was backed by which Spanish rulers?

Q10 Who invented the spinning jenny?

Q1 Which gang were the victims of the 1929 Saint Valentine's Day Massacre?

Q2 In which war did the Siege of Port Arthur occur?

Q3 Blackbeard was from which English city?

Q4 The Villa Jovis on Capri was built by which Roman emperor?

Q5 The Battle of Bunker Hill was an engagement in which war?

Q6 The *Grete Herball* is what kind of book?

Q7 In what centuries did the Visconti family rule Milan?

Q8 Peter Shore was a Member of Parliament for which British political party?

Q9 What was the capital of the Akkadian Empire?

Q10 Udaipur State was a princely state in which present-day country?

<u>**General History 26 (average)**</u>

Q1 Which political ideology heavily influenced the work of historian Eric Hobsbawm?

Q2 Which agreement preceded the United States Constitution?

Q3 Which two cities was the RMS *Titanic* sailing between on its fateful maiden voyage?

Q4 Who named nitrous oxide 'laughing gas'?

Q5 In what year was the Nobel Prize first awarded?

Q6 Who was the first First Lady of the United States?

Q7 *The Prince* was a political treatise written by who?

Q8 What was the Ottoman Sultan Suleiman I's nickname?

Q9 The physician Paracelsus was a key figure in which country's Renaissance?

Q10 Thomas Hobbes is best known for writing which book?

Q1 What is inscribed in Roman numerals on the tabula ansata held in the left hand of the Statue of Liberty?

Q2 The Congo Free State was ruled personally by which Belgian monarch?

Q3 The *Hindenburg* airship exploded over which US state in 1937?

Q4 Which Mexican revolutionary was assassinated in 1923?

Q5 What is the name of the model village John Cadbury had built for his workers?

Q6 Compared with the Roman Empire, how large was the Mongol Empire at the time of Genghis Khan's death?

Q7 How many Vice Presidents served under Franklin Roosevelt?

Q8 The Council of Trent was prompted by which schism in the Catholic Church?

Q9 What was France's first settlement in North America?

Q10 The Bell Witch Haunting is a legend originating from which US state?

<u>**General History 28 (average)**</u>

Q1 *The Arrival of a Train at La Ciotat Station* was a short film directed by which brothers?

Q2 What is the largest building in Teotihuacan?

Q3 The Rwandan genocide involved which two ethnic groups?

Q4 Which year marked the end of British rule on the Indian subcontinent?

Q5 Which city became capital of West Germany in 1949?

Q6 In what year was the Treaty of Ghent, ending the War of 1812, signed?

Q7 Which saint was the first recorded British martyr?

Q8 Who led Vichy France?

Q9 The biblical Magi are better known by what name?

Q10 Jean-Baptiste Colbert was a key advisor to which French king?

<u>**General History 29 (average)**</u>

Q1 Who was Horatio Nelson's deputy during the Battle of Trafalgar 1805?

Q2 The 'man in the iron mask' is commonly associated with which French King?

Q3 Hannibal Barca was a general from which Phoenician state?

Q4 Who became the first President of Haiti in 1801?

Q5 Eugene Botkin was famously the physician of who?

Q6 Who was the first person to enter outer space?

Q7 The lighthouse Smeaton's Tower is in which city?

Q8 Francisco Pizarro led the expedition that conquered which empire?

Q9 The creation of the Commonwealth of Independent States followed the dissolution of which union?

Q10 The *Standart* was the royal yacht of which monarch?

General History 30 (average)

Q1 Which intelligence agency preceded the Central Intelligence Agency (CIA)?

Q2 What was the Roman name for France?

Q3 In what year was the first modern Olympic Games held?

Q4 Which three members of the House of York became King of England?

Q5 Who married both Louis VII of France and Henry II of England?

Q6 The Rapa Nui are the native Polynesian inhabitants of which island?

Q7 The *Rocket* was a steam locomotive designed by which engineer?

Q8 Thomas Aquinas was a member of which Catholic religious order?

Q9 In which English town did Sake Dean Mahomed die?

Q10 The doge was the most senior elected official in which two Italian republics?

General History 31 (average)

Q1 The Heptarchy was unified to form which kingdom in the 10th century?

Q2 Was there a set number of crusades?

Q3 Who was the first European explorer to sail around the Cape of Good Hope?

Q4 Cato the Younger was an opponent of which famous dictator?

Q5 Before being renamed by the Turks, what was Istanbul called?

Q6 Which English explorer was executed in 1618?

Q7 In what year was the British Broadcasting Corporation (BBC) founded?

Q8 The Battle of the Catalaunian Plains led to the Huns withdrawing from which region of the Roman Empire?

Q9 In which country was gunpowder invented?

Q10 Henry the Navigator was the fourth son of which Portuguese king?

Q1 What class of ship was the RMS *Titanic*?

Q2 What was the Roman name for London?

Q3 Masyaf Castle was home to which sect?

Q4 Who succeeded Abraham Lincoln as president?

Q5 Which Scottish king was killed by a cannon in 1460?

Q6 What was Babe Ruth's real name?

Q7 Ibn Khaldun was a leading Arab scholar in which field?

Q8 What was the first public railway to use steam locomotives?

Q9 What did the British gain from their victory at the Battle of the Plains of Abraham?

Q10 A major slave rebellion broke out in which French colony in 1791?

Q1 Under which monarch did England lose its last territorial possession in France, Calais?

Q2 Joseph Merrick, often incorrectly called John Merrick, was known by what nickname?

Q3 Which US president mediated the peace negotiations to end the Russo-Japanese War?

Q4 Who was the first King of Belgium?

Q5 Who invented Coca-Cola?

Q6 What was the occupation of Albert Speer?

Q7 The Sutton Hoo burial site is located in which English county?

Q8 What illness did baseball player Lou Gehrig die from?

Q9 The *Cutty Sark* was what kind of ship?

Q10 Present-day Vietnam was part of which French colony?

<u>General History 34 (average)</u>

Q1 The Great Fire of London 1666 started in what street?

Q2 Who was the first person to circumnavigate the world?

Q3 Which Chinese dynasty followed the Ch'in Dynasty?

Q4 Who was the first person to reach the summit of Mount Everest?

Q5 Which ice hockey great was nicknamed Mr Hockey?

Q6 Where was the Great Exhibition of 1851 held?

Q7 The sackbut was a precursor to which musical instrument?

Q8 Huldrych Zwingli was a leader of the Protestant Reformation in what country?

Q9 Which company's tea was destroyed at the Boston Tea Party?

Q10 The play *Cato, a Tragedy* is based on the last days of which Roman statesman?

General History 35 (average)

Q1 Who was the first Prime Minister of the United Kingdom?

Q2 Who is the only United States president to serve non-consecutive terms?

Q3 Which lasted longer: the Eastern or Western Roman Empire?

Q4 What was formerly built on the site of Tokyo Imperial Palace?

Q5 What did Granville Sharp campaign for the abolition of?

Q6 Maximilian I of Mexico was the younger brother of which Emperor?

Q7 The Monroe Doctrine took effect in what year?

Q8 In what year was the Organization of American States founded?

Q9 Who is credited with establishing Sweden as a great power?

Q10 William of Malmesbury was the foremost English historian of which century?

<u>**General History 36 (expert)**</u>

Q1 Fernand Braudel was a leader of which school of history?

Q2 In what year did Constantinople fall to the Turks?

Q3 In what field did George Cruikshank reach an international audience?

Q4 What was the name of the plantation John Rolfe established in the Virginia Colony?

Q5 Which shipbuilding company built the RMS *Titanic*?

Q6 Who was the first President of the Canadian Pacific Railway?

Q7 The British invasions of the River Plate refers to a series of unsuccessful British attempts to seize control of parts of which Spanish Viceroyalty?

Q8 Which 1846 revolt led to California declaring itself an independent republic?

Q9 The Ise Grand Shrine is dedicated which Shinto goddess?

Q10 The Long March was a military retreat undertaken by which army?

<u>**General History 37 (expert)**</u>

Q1 What was Billy the Kid's birth name?

Q2 Salamis and Mycale were battles fought in which war?

Q3 What was the capital city of the Umayyad Caliphate?

Q4 Pocahontas was the daughter of which chief?

Q5 In what year was the controversial Stamp Act of 1765 repealed?

Q6 Tecumseh was a member of which North American tribe?

Q7 The Good Neighbour policy was the foreign policy of President Franklin Roosevelt's administration towards which region?

Q8 Which admiral led the Japanese to victory at the Battle of Tsushima?

Q9 Who designed the advertisement *Lord Kitchener Wants You*?

Q10 Gabriele D'Annunzio is associated with which 19th century literary movement?

<u>**General History 38 (expert)**</u>

Q1 Who attempted to assassinate President Andrew Jackson in 1835?

Q2 Which prophet founded Manichaeism in the 3rd century AD?

Q3 Which German count invented the zeppelin?

Q4 In which country did King Hassan II ascend the throne in 1961?

Q5 In what year were the Henry Wood Promenade Concerts, otherwise known as the Proms, founded?

Q6 Which group were the victims of the St. Bartholomew's Day massacre?

Q7 What does the term 'the peculiar institution' refer to?

Q8 In European folklore and mythology a Melusine is a spirit of what?

Q9 Nader Shah defeated the army of Mughal Emperor Muhammad Shah at which battle in 1739?

Q10 Muhammad Ali of Egypt was a member of what ethnic group?

General History 39 (expert)

Q1 Which ship was Horatio Nelson's favourite?

Q2 What was the ceremonial capital of the Achaemenid Empire?

Q3 The Three Mile Island accident occurred in 1979 in which US state?

Q4 What was the nationality of Paul Gorguloff, who assassinated French President Paul Doumer in 1932?

Q5 Which deity is Captain James Cook believed to have been mistakenly identified as by native inhabitants of Hawaii?

Q6 What is Peter Carl Fabergé best known for?

Q7 The monk Iliodor was an enemy of which self-proclaimed holy man?

Q8 What was the nickname of the Frankish king, Pepin III?

Q9 Edward the Exile, the son of Edmund Ironside, spent most of his life in exile in which kingdom?

Q10 Ignatius of Loyola founded which religious order?

Q1 Bull-leaping is thought to have been a key ritual in which Bronze Age civilisation?

Q2 Who was the first President of the Republic of Ireland?

Q3 During which war did the Battle of Blenheim take place?

Q4 Anna Vyrubova was a close friend of which member of the Russian royal family?

Q5 Which American battleship sunk in Havana Harbour during the Cuban revolt against Spain?

Q6 What was Genghis Khan's religion?

Q7 Who succeeded Frederick Barbarossa as Holy Roman Emperor?

Q8 Isambard Kingdom Brunel is associated with which railway company?

Q9 *Curia regis* is a Latin term meaning what?

Q10 What was the role of Harry Burton during the excavation of Tutankhamun's tomb?

<u>**General History 41 (expert)**</u>

Q1 What was the principal religion of the Achaemenid Empire?

Q2 Which Scottish King died at the Battle of Flodden in 1513?

Q3 What was *Titanic* survivor Molly Brown nicknamed?

Q4 Where was the first Benedictine monastery established?

Q5 How many popes resided in Avignon between 1309 and 1376?

Q6 The physician Andreas Vesalius was a professor at which university?

Q7 The Stone of Scone was originally used for the coronation of monarchs from which kingdom?

Q8 In what year was the Canadian Pacific Railway completed?

Q9 Which famous author published *The Jungle* in 1904?

Q10 Which leaders were known as the Big Four at the Paris Peace Conference in 1919?

Q1 In what year was the Suez Canal opened?

Q2 What is the name of the wall that the Romans built north of Hadrian's Wall?

Q3 What was the nickname of the Canadian ice hockey player Maurice Richard?

Q4 Which pope did Napoleon take prisoner in 1798?

Q5 Who founded the Timurid Empire?

Q6 Cluny Abbey was known for its strict adherence to which text?

Q7 The Montreal Canadiens, the longest continuously operating professional ice hockey team in the world, were founded in what year?

Q8 The House of Sforza were based in which duchy?

Q9 René Descartes is generally considered to be one of the most notable intellectual figures of which golden age?

Q10 The Battle of Cajamarca resulted in the capture of who?

<u>**General History 43 (expert)**</u>

Q1 Thucydides wrote a history of which war?

Q2 In what year was Oxford University established?

Q3 Which battle was the final confrontation in the Jacobite rising of 1745?

Q4 The Cod Wars refers to a series of confrontations between which two countries over fishing rights?

Q5 Who was the first elected female head of government in modern history?

Q6 The Black Hand secret military society sought to undermine which empire?

Q7 Bahram V, Shah of the Sasanian Empire, fought wars against the Hephthalites and which empire?

Q8 Stepan Timofeyevich Razin, the leader of a major uprising against tsarist bureaucracy in Russia, was a member of which East-Slavic-speaking people?

Q9 Who is the only person to have served as governor of two US states?

Q10 Edward the Martyr was the eldest son of which English king?

Q1 What were the four Panhellenic Games?

Q2 What was Homs formerly called?

Q3 Name the seven wonders of the ancient world.

Q4 John Watts was a founder of which joint-stock company?

Q5 What was the name of the first female flight attendant?

Q6 What part of his anatomy did Tycho Brahe lose after fighting a duel?

Q7 What social class did the Roman historian Suetonius belong to?

Q8 Who commissioned the construction of Hōryū-ji temple?

Q9 Who composed the work *Oration on the Dignity of Man* in 1486?

Q10 The Nile Expedition (1884-85) was a British mission to relieve which Major-General's forces?

<u>**General History 45 (expert)**</u>

Q1 Which Chicago hotel was Al Capone's primary residence between 1928 and 1931?

Q2 Chandragupta II was one of the most powerful emperors of which empire?

Q3 The Battle of Tsushima took place during which war?

Q4 Who commissioned the *Vita Ædwardi Regis* (*Life of King Edward*)?

Q5 Which monarch was killed at the Battle of Lützen?

Q6 James Wolfe faced which French commander at the Battle of the Plains of Abraham?

Q7 Cao Futian was a leader of which secret society?

Q8 Cecil Rhodes was Prime Minister of which British colony?

Q9 John D. Rockefeller founded which oil company?

Q10 Who conducted the first circumnavigation of Australia?

Q1 The period of the Gupta Empire, from AD 320 to 530, is generally regarded as what in relation to India's history?

Q2 Between what years was the Trans-Siberian Railway built?

Q3 How many popes have been named Pius?

Q4 Which bird species, last sighted off the coast of Iceland, became extinct in the mid-nineteenth century?

Q5 The historian Bernard Pares's work focused on which country?

Q6 The name of the Buddhist temple Kinkaku-ji can be translated into English as meaning what?

Q7 What was the profession of Matthew Hopkins?

Q8 Who were the 'Big Four' railway companies in the United Kingdom from 1923-47?

Q9 Sebastião José de Carvalho e Melo, Marquis of Pombal was a powerful political figure in which country?

Q10 The *Kangxi Dictionary* was the standard dictionary in the 18th and 19th centuries in which country?

Q1 Who was the founder of modern source-based history?

Q2 According to Greek mythology, how did Athena come into being?

Q3 James B. Donovan negotiated the exchange of Soviet spy Rudolf Abel for which American pilot?

Q4 Which 6th century historian wrote the *History of the Franks*?

Q5 The death of Charles George Gordon is romanticised in a painting by which artist?

Q6 The Uruguayan Civil War was known by what name in Spanish?

Q7 In what year was the Ford Model T first produced?

Q8 Who ruled Mexico during the *porfiriato*?

Q9 The Delhi Durbar was held three times to mark what?

Q10 László Rajk held what position in the Hungarian government between 1946 and 1948?

<u>**General History 48 (expert)**</u>

Q1 The Lion Gate was the main entrance to which Bronze Age citadel?

Q2 What two colours were on the Kingdom of Mercia's flag?

Q3 In what year was oil discovered in Iran?

Q4 The statesman George Macartney described the British Empire as 'this vast empire on which the sun never sets, and whose bounds nature has not yet ascertained' following which war?

Q5 Which two Italian-American anarchists were executed on 23rd August 1927?

Q6 The Tennessee-based teacher John Thomas Scopes was charged with violating which act?

Q7 Henry Ford established which town in the Amazon Rainforest?

Q8 James Walter McCord Jr. was involved in which political scandal?

Q9 Which democratically elected president was ousted (with American support) in 1973?

Q10 Which state existed between 1967 and 1970, during the Nigerian Civil War?

<u>**General History 49 (expert)**</u>

Q1 Who is the youngest non-commissioned officer in the history of the United States Army?

Q2 The Treasury of Atreus is what type of tomb?

Q3 The Football War, in 1969, was fought between which two countries?

Q4 Who is the semi-legendary founder of the Merovingian dynasty?

Q5 Which Viking was the first Duke of Normandy?

Q6 Who was the first Indian to publish a book in English?

Q7 Voltaire criticised the execution of the Protestant merchant Jean Calas in what 1763 work?

Q8 Kashmere Gate was built by which Mughal Emperor?

Q9 The son of Queen Anne of Great Britain, Prince William, Duke of Gloucester, was a member of which royal house?

Q10 Which palace was the seat of the first Russian Parliament (Duma)?

<u>**General History 50 (expert)**</u>

Q1 What was the name of Horatio Nelson's mistress?

Q2 Who was America named after?

Q3 Mount Penglai is a legendary land in which country's mythology?

Q4 The political treatise *Defensor pacis* was written by which Italian scholar?

Q5 The two failed Mongol invasions of Japan took place in which years?

Q6 According to the *Book of Genesis* and *Books of Chronicles*, Nimrod was a great-grandson of which famous Biblical figure?

Q7 Abigail Masham was a favourite of which British monarch?

Q8 The Treaty of Tientsin was signed during which war?

Q9 The United States Army Special Forces started wearing what kind of headgear under President Kennedy?

Q10 Winston Churchill had a tattoo of what?

Battles and

Wars

<u>**Greco-Persian Wars 1 (easy)**</u>

Q1 Who was King of Persia at the start of the Greco-Persian Wars?

A Xerxes I
B Cambyses II
C Bahram V
D Darius the Great

Q2 The first Persian invasion of Greece ended with which battle?

A Battle of Marathon
B Battle of Salamis
C Battle of the Granicus
D Battle of Aegospotami

Q3 Who was Mardonius?

A A king
B A military commander
C A chronicler
D An artist

Q4 The Battle of Salamis was fought on what kind of terrain?

A Plains
B Sea
C Mountains
D Forest

Q5 The Battle of Mycale took place on what mountain?

A Vesuvius
B Olympus
C Mycale
D Pindus

Q6 Pausanias was a general from which Greek city state?

    A Athens
    B Sparta
    C Argos
    D Corinth

Q7 Some historical sources say the Greco-Persian Wars were ended by the signing of which treaty?

    A Treaty of Tordesillas
    B Treaty of Versailles
    C Peace of Westphalia
    D Peace of Callias

Q8 The *sparabara* were what in the Achaemenid Empire?

    A Battleships
    B Infantry
    C Colonial administrators
    D Farmers

Q9 The phalanx was a type of what?

    A Horse saddle
    B Military formation
    C Ship sail
    D Chariot

Q10 After the Peloponnesian War, which Greek city state became dominant?

    A Athens
    B Argos
    C Sparta
    D Corinth

<u>**Greco-Persian Wars 2 (average)**</u>

Q1 In what year did the Greco-Persian Wars break out?

Q2 Who won the Greco-Persian Wars?

Q3 Who was victorious at the Siege of Eretria?

Q4 Which Persian King launched the second Persian invasion of Greece?

Q5 Who led the Greek city states' forces at the Battle of Thermopylae?

Q6 What was the name of the association of Greek city states that was formed in 478 BC?

Q7 Themistocles relied on the support of which section of Athenian society?

Q8 Xanthippus was a politician from which Greek city state?

Q9 Which series of wars followed the second Persian invasion of Greece?

Q10 Cimon died on what island?

Greco-Persian Wars 3 (expert)

Q1 The Siege of Naxos was a failed attempt by who to conquer the island of Naxos?

Q2 Which revolt occurred between 499–493 BC?

Q3 Who is reported to have assassinated Xerxes I of Persia?

Q4 Who led the Delian League's forces at the Battle of the Eurymedon?

Q5 What were hoplites in the Greek city states?

Q6 What was the final land battle during the second Persian invasion of Greece?

Q7 The Ten Thousand were a force of predominantly Greek mercenary units employed by who?

Q8 Which two city states helped Aristagoras capture and burn the Persian regional capital of Sardis in 498 BC?

Q9 Datis is remembered for commanding the Persian forces with who else?

Q10 Which city state was the dominant power in the Delian League?

The Punic Wars (average)

Q1 The Punic Wars were fought between Rome and which other state?

Q2 How many Punic Wars were there?

Q3 Hannibal's crossing of the Alps occurred during which of the Punic Wars?

Q4 Which other series of wars ran concurrently with the Punic Wars?

Q5 At the end of the Punic Wars, Rome emerged as the dominant power in which region?

Q6 The First Punic War began as a local conflict between the Mamertines of Messina and who?

Q7 Who won the Battle of the Bagradas River (255 BC)?

Q8 Who led the Romans to victory at the Battle of Zama?

Q9 What was the last major battle of the Punic Wars?

Q10 The term *'Carthago delenda est'* originates from just before which war?

<u>**Norman Conquest 1 (easy)**</u>

Q1 The death of which king triggered a succession crisis in England in 1066?

    A Alfred the Great
    B Edward the Confessor
    C Harold Godwinson
    D William the Conqueror

Q2 What was William I of England's primary title before becoming King of England?

    A King of France
    B Duke of Brittany
    C Earl of Suffolk
    D Duke of Normandy

Q3 What was the name of the 'Great Survey' of England and parts of Wales, carried out after the conquest and completed in 1086?

    A Domesday Book
    B Beveridge Report
    C Magana Carta
    D *Leges barbarorum*

Q4 How long was Harold Godwinson King of England?

    A Less than a year
    B 2 years
    C 5 years
    D 10 years

Q5 What body of water did William I cross in his conquest of England?

    A Bering Strait
    B Irish Sea
    C English Channel
    D North Sea

Q6 Who did the English fight at the Battle of Hastings?

    A Welsh
    B Vikings
    C French
    D Normans

Q7 At the Battle of Hastings, Harold Godwinson is said to have been hit by an arrow. Which body part did it allegedly strike?

    A Eye
    B Heart
    C Hip
    D Neck

Q8 Which cultural group controlled England prior to the Norman Conquest?

    A Picts
    B Romans
    C Anglo-Saxons
    D Franks

Q9 Which kingdom prevailed at the Battle of Fulford?

    A Kingdom of England
    B Kingdom of France
    C Kingdom of Scotland
    D Kingdom of Norway

Q10 How was Harold Godwinson related to Gyrth Godwinson and Leofwine Godwinson?

    A Uncle
    B Cousin
    C Brother
    D Father

<u>**Norman Conquest 2 (average)**</u>

Q1 Who did Harold Godwinson beat at the Battle of Stamford Bridge before marching south to fight the Battle of Hastings?

Q2 Which part of the Tower of London was built on William I's orders?

Q3 What is the name of the tapestry which depicts the events leading up to the Norman conquest of England?

Q4 Who was Archbishop of Canterbury at the time of the Norman Conquest?

Q5 Tostig Godwinson supported whose attempted conquest of England?

Q6 On which hill did Harold Godwinson form a defensive position before the Battle of Hastings?

Q7 On what day in 1066 did the Battle of Hastings occur?

Q8 Baile Hill is located near which city?

Q9 Which Count of Boulogne fought on the Norman side at the Battle of Hastings?

Q10 The Danegeld was a tax raised to pay tribute to who?

<u>**Norman Conquest 3 (expert)**</u>

Q1 Who chronicled the Norman Conquest of England in *The Deeds of William, Duke of Normandy and King of England*?

Q2 Which abbey claims to be the site of Harold Godwinson's secret burial?

Q3 Eadric the Wild, who led English resistance to the Norman Conquest, was a magnate from which region of England?

Q4 Out of Harald Hardrada's 300 ships, how many of them returned to Norway?

Q5 Edgar Ætheling was elected King of England by which political institution in 1066?

Q6 Before 1066, a *fyrd* was a type of what?

Q7 Who was the last Anglo-Saxon earl to be executed during the reign of William I?

Q8 In what year did the Siege of Exeter occur?

Q9 In what year did the Revolt of the Earls occur?

Q10 In which century was the term 'Norman yoke' first used?

<u>**First Crusade 1 (easy)**</u>

Q1 In what year was Jerusalem seized by the Crusaders?

   A 1089
   B 1091
   C 1099
   D 1100

Q2 Under which pope did the First Crusade begin?

   A Urban II
   B Pius IV
   C Paul III
   D Gregory I

Q3 Peter the Hermit was a priest from which town?

   A Vannes
   B Quiberon
   C Amiens
   D St Etienne

Q4 In what year did the People's Crusade occur?

   A 1090
   B 1096
   C 1100
   D 1102

Q5 Who served as the first King of Jerusalem?

   A Richard I
   B Philip II
   C Baldwin I
   D Robert Curthose

Q6 Which city fell to the Crusaders in June 1098?

> **A** Jerusalem
> **B** Acre
> **C** Damascus
> **D** Antioch

Q7 The Muslim conquest of the Levant took place in what century?

> **A** 5th
> **B** 7th
> **C** 9th
> **D** 11th

Q8 Who was the Seljuq Sultan of Rûm during the First Crusade?

> **A** Saladin
> **B** Malik Shah
> **C** Kilij Arslan I
> **D** Suleiman ibn Qutulmish

Q9 Yağısıyan was loyal to which empire?

> **A** Mongol Empire
> **B** Ottoman Empire
> **C** Achaemenid Empire
> **D** Seljuk Empire

Q10 Which group were victims of the Rhineland massacres?

> **A** Jews
> **B** Huguenots
> **C** Muslims
> **D** Catholics

<u>**First Crusade 2 (average)**</u>

Q1 *Deus vult*, a phrase commonly associated with the First Crusade, means what in English?

Q2 Which two crusader states were founded in 1098?

Q3 Who was the Byzantine Emperor at the time of the First Crusade?

Q4 The Battle of Ascalon involved a futile attempt by the Saracens to do what?

Q5 Which Duke of Normandy served at the Battle of Dorylaeum?

Q6 Where did the Muslim governor of Jerusalem surrender to the Crusaders?

Q7 In what years did the First Crusade take place?

Q8 Which caliphate was in charge of Jerusalem at the time of the First Crusade?

Q9 The priest Fulcher of Chartres served which king?

Q10 Which major event in the history of Christianity took place a few decades prior to the First Crusade?

<u>First Crusade 3 (expert)</u>

Q1 At which council was the call to arms made, which ultimately resulted in the First Crusade?

Q2 In what year did the Siege of Nicaea occur?

Q3 The Crusaders reportedly resorted to what after capturing the town of Ma'arrat al-Numan?

Q4 Who was governor of Jerusalem when it fell to the Crusaders?

Q5 Raymond IV was Count of which Crusader state?

Q6 What was Guglielmo Embriaco's occupation?

Q7 Who wrote the *Historia Hierosolymitana*?

Q8 Which minor crusade followed the First Crusade?

Q9 What was Walter Sans Avoir mistakenly known as?

Q10 Thoros of Edessa practiced which faith?

Third Crusade 1 (easy)

Q1 Saladin ruled which dynasty?

    A Umayyad
    B Rashidun
    C Ottoman
    D Ayyubid

Q2 Which kingdom was established after the Third Crusade?

    A Kingdom of Jerusalem
    B Kingdom of Cyprus
    C Kingdom of Bulgaria
    D Kingdom of Tlemcen

Q3 The Battle of Philomelion took place on which peninsula?

    A Balkan
    B Crimean
    C Anatolian
    D Iberian

Q4 Who launched the Crusade of 1197?

    A Richard I of England
    B Henry VI, Holy Roman Emperor
    C Philip II of France
    D Valdemar II of Denmark

Q5 How did Henry II, Count of Champagne die?

    A Old age
    B In battle
    C Fell out a window
    D Poison

Q6 The *Itinerarium Regis Ricardi* is written in what language?

A Latin
B Greek
C French
D Hebrew

Q7 What was the name of the Byzantine Emperor who sought to form an alliance with Saladin?

A Isaac II Angelos
B Michael VII Doukas
C Romanos IV Diogenes
D Alexios II Komnenos

Q8 The Battle of Iconium took place in what year?

A 1187
B 1190
C 1192
D 1198

Q9 Conrad of Montferrat was born in which present-day country?

A France
B Spain
C Germany
D Italy

Q10 In what year did Sibylla, Queen of Jerusalem die?

A 1187
B 1188
C 1190
D 1194

Q1 What disease did Baldwin IV of Jerusalem suffer from?

Q2 Which French king was involved in the Third Crusade?

Q3 What triggered the Third Crusade?

Q4 What happened to the Holy Roman Emperor, Frederick I that prevented him from reaching the Holy Land?

Q5 Which treaty ended the Third Crusade?

Q6 Richard de Camville was a senior military commander of which king?

Q7 Where was the juvenile King of Jerusalem, Baldwin V buried?

Q8 Which side did Leo I, King of Armenia support during the Third Crusade?

Q9 Frederick VI, Duke of Swabia died during which siege?

Q10 Baha ad-Din ibn Shaddad is known for writing a biography of who?

<u>**Third Crusade 3 (expert)**</u>

Q1 In what year did the Battle of Hattin take place?

Q2 Who issued the papal bull *Audita tremendi* calling for the Third Crusade?

Q3 Who was Archbishop of Canterbury when the Third Crusade began?

Q4 Before his execution in 1189, what position did Gerard de Ridefort hold?

Q5 In what years did the Siege of Acre occur?

Q6 Richard I broke off a long-standing betrothal to who in order to marry Berengaria of Navarre?

Q7 In what year did Philip II of France leave the Holy Land?

Q8 Who defeated Saladin at the Battle of Montgisard (1177)?

Q9 From which English town did Richard I's army depart for the Holy Land?

Q10 Which battle took place on 7 September 1191?

Hundred Years' War 1 (easy)

Q1 How many years did the Hundred Years' War last?

    A 99
    B 100
    C 116
    D 130

Q2 How many English kings were involved in the Hundred Years' War?

    A 1
    B 3
    C 5
    D 7

Q3 How was Philip VI of France related to his predecessor, Charles IV?

    A Son
    B Brother
    C Brother-in-law
    D Cousin

Q4 Which major battle took place in 1415?

    A Battle of Agincourt
    B Battle of Crécy
    C Battle of Poitiers
    D Battle of Castillon

Q5 Who launched the Loire Campaign?

    A Charles VII of France
    B Henry VI of England
    C Joan of Arc
    D Jean de Brosse

Q6 Which weapon was essential to numerous English victories in the Hundred Years' War?

    A Sword
    B Longbow
    C Trebuchet
    D Greek fire

Q7 The Black Prince was a key commander during which English king's reign?

    A Edward III
    B Richard II
    C Henry IV
    D Henry V

Q8 Who was captured at the Battle of Neville's Cross?

    A Joan of Arc
    B Henry VI of France
    C Henry VI of England
    D David II of Scotland

Q9 Which royal house ruled France during the Hundred Years' War?

    A House of Bourbon
    B House of Valois
    C House of Burgundy
    D House of Anjou

Q10 Which treaty was agreed between England and France in 1359?

    A Treaty of Paris
    B Treaty of the Kings
    C Treaty of London
    D Treaty of Bruges

<u>**Hundred Years' War 2 (average)**</u>

Q1 What key issue was the Hundred Years' War fought over?

Q2 How many French kings were involved in the Hundred Years' War?

Q3 Who was the closest male relative to Charles IV of France when he died?

Q4 Which kingdom ultimately emerged victorious in the Hundred Years' War?

Q5 Which battle is widely considered to mark the end of the Hundred Years' War?

Q6 The Treaty of Troyes was agreed between which two kings?

Q7 At which 1430 siege was Joan of Arc captured?

Q8 England's loss of continental holdings during the Hundred Years' War is often viewed as a key cause of which civil war?

Q9 Which Europe-wide crisis struck in the early stages of the Hundred Years' War?

Q10 Who led the English forces at the Battle of Poitiers?

<u>**Hundred Years' War 3 (expert)**</u>

Q1 Which three phases is the Hundred Years' War commonly divided into by historians?

Q2 Which key English nobleman was slain at the Battle of Castillon?

Q3 In what year was the Battle of Patay fought?

Q4 Which 1424 battle was regarded by the English as a second Agincourt?

Q5 Which village was the birthplace of Joan of Arc?

Q6 The Congress of Arras was attended by representatives of which three states?

Q7 What event claimed the lives of an estimated 1,000 English soldiers on Black Monday (1360)?

Q8 In what year did the Battle of Crécy take place?

Q9 What campaign took place between 1359 and 1360?

Q10 The Truce of Leulinghem was agreed between which two kings?

Wars of the Roses 1 (easy)

Q1 The Wars of the Roses took place in which kingdom?

  A Kingdom of France
  B Kingdom of Aragon
  C Kingdom of Poland
  D Kingdom of England

Q2 The Wars of the Roses resulted from a split in which royal house?

  A Stuart
  B Blois
  C Plantagenet
  D Tudor

Q3 How many Yorkist kings of England were there?

  A 2
  B 3
  C 4
  D 5

Q4 What was the last significant battle of the Wars of the Roses?

  A Battle of Towton
  B Battle of Wakefield
  C Battle of Tewkesbury
  D Battle of Bosworth Field

Q5 In which century did the Wars of the Roses occur?

  A 11th
  B 13th
  C 15th
  D 16th

Q6 Under which king's rule did the Wars of the Roses break out?

    A Richard II
    B Richard III
    C Henry V
    D Henry VI

Q7 What coloured rose is the House of York associated with?

    A White
    B Red
    C Yellow
    D Black

Q8 The Battle of Blore Heath was fought in which county?

    A Rutland
    B Herefordshire
    C Staffordshire
    D Shropshire

Q9 Robin of Redesdale led an uprising against which king?

    A Edward IV
    B Edward V
    C Richard II
    D Henry IV

Q10 Who was captured at the Battle of Northampton?

    A Richard III
    B Henry VI
    C Edward IV
    D Edward V

<u>**Wars of the Roses 2 (average)**</u>

Q1 The Wars of the Roses involved a conflict between which two royal houses?

Q2 Which marriage essentially ended the Wars of the Roses?

Q3 Which battle is widely regarded as marking the beginning of the Wars of the Roses?

Q4 What title did Edward IV's father hold?

Q5 What were the names of the Princes in the Tower?

Q6 Where is Henry VI believed to have been murdered?

Q7 Which nobleman was known as the 'Kingmaker'?

Q8 Which series of books by George R. R. Martin was inspired by the Wars of the Roses?

Q9 What was Richard III's title before he became King of England?

Q10 How many kings did Thomas Bourchier crown?

<u>**Wars of the Roses 3 (expert)**</u>

Q1 Richard, Duke of York and which other notable figure was slain at the Battle of Wakefield?

Q2 At which battle was Richard Neville, Earl of Warwick killed?

Q3 In what year was Henry VI briefly restored to the throne?

Q4 In what year did Henry VII become King of England?

Q5 Which Act of Parliament justified Richard III's claim to the throne?

Q6 The Battle of Stoke Field was fought between Henry VII and which pretender?

Q7 John Everett Millais painted a famous portrait of who?

Q8 What was Perkin Warbeck's nationality?

Q9 Jasper Tudor was what relation to Henry VII?

Q10 The Battle of Edgecote Moor was fought in what year?

<u>**Thirty Years' War 1 (easy)**</u>

Q1 On which continent did the Thirty Years' War take place?

    A Africa
    B Asia
    C Europe
    D North America

Q2 Who formed the Protestant Union in 1608?

    A Frederick IV, Elector Palatine
    B James I of England
    C Albrecht von Wallenstein
    D Johann Tserclaes, Count of Tilly

Q3 Who was Holy Roman Emperor when the Thirty Years' War broke out?

    A Matthias
    B Ferdinand II
    C Ferdinand III
    D Joseph I

Q4 The Old Town Square execution took place in which city?

    A Vienna
    B Paris
    C Munich
    D Prague

Q5 Frederick V of the Palatinate briefly served as King of what?

    A England
    B France
    C Bohemia
    D Prussia

Q6 Which country regained its independence during the Thirty Years' War?

A Scotland
B Austria
C Belgium
D Portugal

Q7 What was Dorothea Flock convicted of?

A Treason
B Murder
C Witchcraft
D Heresy

Q8 What was Drudenhaus?

A A military honour
B A prison
C A fortress
D A prayer

Q9 The House of Habsburg ruled over which two countries during the Thirty Years' War?

A Spain and France
B France and Portugal
C Spain and Austria
D Austria and Greece

Q10 France and Spain were still at war after the Thirty Years' War had finished. When did the Franco-Spanish War end?

A 1649
B 1652
C 1659
D 1700

Q1 Albrecht von Wallenstein was a military leader from which kingdom?

Q2 What is the name of the series of treaties which brought the Thirty Years' War to an end?

Q3 The Thirty Years' War involved a conflict between which two branches of Christianity?

Q4 The Peace of Augsburg allowed rulers within the Holy Roman Empire to choose between which two branches of Christianity as their official religion?

Q5 Which majority Catholic nation fought against the Catholic Hapsburg dynasty from 1635 until the end of the Thirty Years' War?

Q6 The king of which country was killed at the Battle of Lützen?

Q7 The Treaty of Bärwalde formed an alliance between which two countries?

Q8 How was Charles I of England related to Frederick V, Elector Palatine?

Q9 The Eight Years' War resulted in the independence of the Dutch Republic from which empire?

Q10 Which revolt broke out in 1618?

<u>Thirty Years' War 3 (expert)</u>

Q1 In which two cities was the Peace of Westphalia agreed?

Q2 The Battle of White Mountain was fought in what year?

Q3 In the Second Defenestration of Prague, what does the word 'defenestration' refer to?

Q4 What derisive nickname did Frederick V of the Palatinate earn?

Q5 The Edict of Restitution was passed in what year?

Q6 The Peace of Prague (1635) was a peace treaty between the Holy Roman Emperor, Ferdinand II and which other ruler?

Q7 What took place in Bamberg between 1626 and 1631?

Q8 What four major phases can the Thirty Years' War be divided into?

Q9 The Siege of La Rochelle was the result of a war between Louis XIII of France and which ethnoreligious group?

Q10 In what years did the Great Plague of Milan occur?

<u>**English Civil War 1 (easy)**</u>

Q1 What name was given to people loyal to Parliament in the English Civil War?

    A Cavaliers
    B Tories
    C Roundheads
    D Rebels

Q2 The English Civil War involved a rebellion against which English king?

    A James I
    B James II
    C Charles I
    D Charles II

Q3 What did the Kingdom of England become after the fall of the monarchy?

    A English Republic
    B Commonwealth of England
    C English Confederation
    D The Grand Duchy of England

Q4 Who became the first Lord Protector of England?

    A John Hampden
    B Prince Rupert of the Rhine
    C Oliver Cromwell
    D Thomas Fairfax

Q5 The Restoration began in what year?

    A 1649
    B 1656
    C 1660
    D 1666

Q6 Which form of Protestantism did Oliver Cromwell adhere to?

A Anglicanism
B Lutheranism
C Puritanism
D Presbyterianism

Q7 The Short Parliament sat in what year?

A 1635
B 1640
C 1649
D 1650

Q8 How did Thomas Wentworth, Earl of Strafford die?

A Old age
B Poisoning
C In battle
D Execution

Q9 What was the name of Parliament's army?

A The People's Army
B The Templars
C The New Model Army
D The Cromwellians

Q10 Charles II famously hid in a tree near which house?

A Whitwick Manor
B Burghley House
C Blenheim Palace
D Boscobel House

English Civil War 2 (average)

Q1 In what year was Charles I executed?

Q2 The Battle of Worcester ended with the defeat of forces led by who?

Q3 The English Civil War was a part of which series of conflicts?

Q4 Who was commander-in-chief of Parliament's forces?

Q5 Which key battle was fought in June 1645?

Q6 How many English Civil Wars were there?

Q7 The Battle of Edgehill was fought in which county?

Q8 Where did Charles I hold a Parliament between 1644 and 1645?

Q9 What key office did William Laud hold?

Q10 Who was Queen of England during the English Civil War?

<u>English Civil War 3 (expert)</u>

Q1 Who served as the second Lord Protector of England?

Q2 In what year did Pride's Purge occur?

Q3 Which court was established to try Charles I?

Q4 In what years did the Interregnum occur?

Q5 What name was given to the group of cavalry led by Oliver Cromwell?

Q6 Who helped the Parliamentarians win the Battle of Marston Moor?

Q7 What title did Alexander Leslie hold?

Q8 Before Oliver Cromwell became Lord Protector, who governed England?

Q9 Who led the Parliamentarians to victory at the Siege of Hull?

Q10 What was the name of the list of grievances that was presented to Charles I in 1641?

<u>**War of the Spanish Succession (average)**</u>

Q1 In what century did the War of the Spanish Succession take place?

Q2 Which king's death triggered the War of the Spanish Succession?

Q3 Which two alliances fought each other in the War of the Spanish Succession?

Q4 Which states signed the Treaty of Baden?

Q5 In what years were the series of peace treaties known collectively as the Peace of Utrecht signed?

Q6 Philip V of Spain was the grandson of which French queen?

Q7 Which three countries signed the Treaty of The Hague (1701)?

Q8 Rákóczi's War of Independence occurred in which Habsburg-controlled kingdom?

Q9 What two territories were ceded to Britain at the end of the War of the Spanish Succession?

Q10 The Barrier Treaties were a series of treaties that created a buffer zone between which two countries?

<u>**American Revolutionary War 1 (easy)**</u>

Q1 Lord Cornwallis surrendered during which siege?

    A Boston
    B Yorktown
    C Vicksburg
    D Tyre

Q2 In what year were the British victorious at the Siege of Charleston?

    A 1776
    B 1778
    C 1780
    D 1783

Q3 Who was King of Great Britain during the American Revolution?

    A George I
    B George II
    C George III
    D George IV

Q4 The Suffolk Resolves was a declaration made by leaders in which colony?

    A Province of Maryland
    B Province of Pennsylvania
    C Province of Massachusetts Bay
    D Delaware Colony

Q5 In which city was the First Continental Congress held?

    A New York City
    B Washington D.C.
    C Charleston
    D Philadelphia

Q6 Jean-Baptiste Donatien de Vimeur was loyal to which country?

A United Kingdom
B USA
C France
D Canada

Q7 In which ocean/sea did the Battle of the Chesapeake take place between the French Navy and the British Royal Navy?

A Atlantic Ocean
B Pacific Ocean
C Mediterranean Sea
D North Sea

Q8 In what year was the Proclamation of Rebellion issued?

A 1773
B 1775
C 1778
D 1783

Q9 The Incident on King Street occurred in which city?

A Philadelphia
B New York City
C Hartford
D Boston

Q10 Who led the Continental Army at the Battle of Trenton?

A Thomas Jefferson
B George Washington
C Charles Lee
D Horatio Gates

Q1 What was the name of the treaty which ended the American Revolutionary War in 1783?

Q2 Who is credited with the American victory at the Battles of Saratoga in 1777?

Q3 How many signatures are there on the Declaration of Independence?

Q4 The Battle of Kings Mountain took place in which US state?

Q5 Who was commander-in-chief of British forces at the start of the American Revolutionary War?

Q6 The Raid of Nassau involved an amphibious assault by Colonial forces against which island?

Q7 Who wrote the pamphlet *Common Sense*, advocating independence from Great Britain?

Q8 Besides from France which two other European nations intervened on behalf of the rebels?

Q9 What were the first military engagements of the American Revolutionary War?

Q10 The Battle of Quebec was fought near which city?

American Revolutionary War 3 (expert)

Q1 Which group aimed to have George Washington replaced as commander-in-chief of the Continental Army between 1777 and 1778?

Q2 What code name was given to the French government's plan to provide the American rebels with military assistance?

Q3 Who commanded the French fleet at the Battle of the Chesapeake?

Q4 The Siege of Savage's Old Fields occurred in which South Carolina town?

Q5 The Continental Congress refused to recognise the legitimacy of which republic throughout the American Revolutionary War?

Q6 In what year did the Capture of Savannah occur?

Q7 Archibald Campbell served as the governor of which American colony?

Q8 Which colony was Nathanael Greene born in?

Q9 In which sea did the Battle of Dogger Bank occur?

Q10 *Washington Crossing the Delaware* is a painting by which artist?

<u>French Revolution 1 (easy)</u>

Q1 What became France's national anthem during the Revolution?

    A God Save the Republic
    B *Vive la liberté!*
    C *La Marseillaise*
    D Star Spangled Banner

Q2 Marie Antoinette was from which country?

    A Austria
    B France
    C Germany
    D Spain

Q3 How long after the Battle of Valmy was the First French Republic declared?

    A 2 days
    B 1 week
    C 2 months
    D 1 year

Q4 Which leader was denounced during the Thermidorian Reaction?

    A Louis XVI
    B Napoleon Bonaparte
    C Maximilien Robespierre
    D Charles de Gaulle

Q5 The French Revolution involved the overthrow of which king?

    A Louis XIV of France
    B Louis XVI of France
    C Charles VIII of France
    D Henry II of France

Q6 By what name is the social and political system that existed prior to the French Revolution known?

    A The Kingship
    B The *Ancien Régime*
    C The Autocracy
    D The Glorious Kingdom

Q7 What city was Jacques Necker from?

    A Geneva
    B Marseilles
    C Paris
    D Nice

Q8 The Declaration of the Rights of Man and of the Citizen was influenced by which American?

    A Patrick Henry
    B George Washington
    C John Adams
    D Thomas Jefferson

Q9 The first written constitution of France was written in what year?

    A 1789
    B 1791
    C 1793
    D 1804

Q10 What country was Axel von Fersen the Younger from?

    A France
    B Norway
    C Sweden
    D Germany

French Revolution 2 (average)

Q1 The 'Reign of Terror' occurred during which years?

Q2 Which series of wars resulted from the French Revolution?

Q3 The National Convention was created after which insurrection?

Q4 In what year was Louis XVI executed?

Q5 The Third Estate refers to what group of people?

Q6 What kind of monarchy ruled the Kingdom of France prior to the French Revolution?

Q7 Members of what took the Tennis Court Oath in 1789?

Q8 Who became King of France after the Bourbon Restoration?

Q9 Which town did Louis XVI famously flee to in 1791?

Q10 What were the Girondins?

<u>**French Revolution 3 (expert)**</u>

Q1 In what year did the Women's March on Versailles occur?

Q2 Maximilien Robespierre was a prominent figure on which committee?

Q3 Who was Governor of the Bastille when it was stormed?

Q4 What new calendar was created during the French Revolution?

Q5 Honoré Gabriel Riqueti was Count of what?

Q6 In what year was the *Fête de la Fédération* first celebrated?

Q7 Georges Danton was a member of what political faction before his death?

Q8 Where was the Declaration of Pilnite issued?

Q9 *L'Ami du peuple* was a newspaper written by who?

Q10 Charlotte Corday was executed for assassinating who?

<u>Napoleonic Wars 1 (easy)</u>

Q1 The Battle of the Three Emperors is also known as what?

    A Battle of Austerlitz
    B Battle of Waterloo
    C Battle of Borodino
    D Battle of Trafalgar

Q2 In what year was Napoleon Bonaparte crowed Emperor of the French?

    A 1789
    B 1793
    C 1800
    D 1804

Q3 Which royal house/dynasty ruled France following the fall of Napoleon?

    A House of Bourbon
    B House of Valois
    C Carolingian Dynasty
    D House of Capet

Q4 Which Russian Tsar led the Sixth Coalition at the Battle of Leipzig?

    A Alexander I
    B Alexander II
    C Nicholas I
    D Nicholas II

Q5 The Continental System was Napoleon's foreign policy against which country?

    A Spain
    B Prussia
    C United Kingdom
    D Sweden

Q6 The French invasion of Russia occurred in what year?

A 1804
B 1812
C 1814
D 1815

Q7 What was the official name of France during the Napoleonic Wars?

A France
B French Republic
C French Empire
D French Confederation

Q8 In which country was the Battle of Borodino fought?

A Russia
B France
C United Kingdom
D Switzerland

Q9 Napoleon and who else signed the Peace of Pressburg?

A William Pitt the Younger
B Pius VII
C Francis II, Holy Roman Emperor
D Maria II of Portugal

Q10 What did Klemens von Metternich offer Napoleon in 1813?

A A Bible
B Unconditional surrender
C Frankfurt proposals
D 10,000 Austrian soldiers

<u>**Napoleonic Wars 2 (average)**</u>

Q1 In what year did the Battle of Waterloo take place?

Q2 What period marked Napoleon's return from exile?

Q3 Francisco Goya produced a number of prints and paintings depicting which war?

Q4 In what years was the War of the Sixth Coalition fought?

Q5 How many coalitions were formed against Napoleon?

Q6 Who did Napoleon declare King of Spain in 1808?

Q7 Which meeting of European diplomats occurred between 1814 and 1815?

Q8 Which 1799 coup brought Napoleon to power?

Q9 The Walcheren Campaign was launched by which country?

Q10 Napoleon's campaign in Egypt resulted in the discovery of which stone?

Napoleonic Wars 3 (expert)

Q1 Which two islands was Napoleon banished to?

Q2 What was the name of the army Napoleon commanded during the Napoleonic Wars?

Q3 Who is believed to have given the order to burn Moscow to the ground in 1812?

Q4 Which twin battles led to the defeat of the Kingdom of Prussia?

Q5 Which French admiral was killed during the Battle of the Nile?

Q6 Which country attacked Copenhagen in the Second Battle of Copenhagen?

Q7 The Battle of Raszyn (1809) was fought in which present-day country?

Q8 Which British army officer was fatally wounded at the Battle of Corunna?

Q9 The Battle of Trafalgar was fought off the coast of which country?

Q10 The formation of the Helvetic Republic was an attempt by the French to impose central authority over which country?

<u>**Crimean War (average)**</u>

Q1 In what years did the Siege of Sevastopol occur?

Q2 In what years was the Crimean War fought?

Q3 Which two empires supported the Ottoman Empire in the Crimean War?

Q4 What type of battle was the Battle of Sinop?

Q5 The Battle of Balaclava took place in what year?

Q6 Which commander led the Charge of the Light Brigade?

Q7 Which nurse is commonly associated with the Crimean War?

Q8 Which treaty ended the Crimean War?

Q9 Which tsars led Russia through the Crimean War?

Q10 What was Roger Fenton's occupation?

<u>**American Civil War 1 (easy)**</u>

Q1 The firing on which fort in 1861 marked the opening of the American Civil War?

    A Fort Sumter
    B Fort Wagner
    C Fort Jackson
    D Fort Harker

Q2 Which state was the first to secede from the Union?

    A North Carolina
    B South Carolina
    C Mississippi
    D Alabama

Q3 What was the first major battle of the American Civil War?

    A First Battle of Bull Run
    B Battle of Shiloh
    C Battle of Antietam
    D Battle of Gettysburg

Q4 Who gave the Gettysburg Address?

    A Ulysses Grant
    B Abraham Lincoln
    C Robert E Lee
    D Stonewall Jackson

Q5 At its peak how many states were there in the Confederate States of America?

    A 5
    B 8
    C 11
    D 19

Q6 Who was President of the Confederate States of America?

   A Alexander Stephens
   B Judah Benjamin
   C John Calhoun
   D Jefferson Davis

Q7 The Siege of Vicksburg took place in which state?

   A Mississippi
   B Virginia
   C Maryland
   D Arkansas

Q8 What era followed the American Civil War?

   A Union Era
   B Era of Good Feelings
   C Progressive Era
   D Reconstruction era

Q9 The Battle of Glorieta Pass was fought in which territory?

   A New Mexico Territory
   B Indian Territory
   C Oregon Territory
   D Idaho Territory

Q10 John Milton Chivington was responsible for which 1864 massacre?

   A Yankee massacre
   B Sand Creek massacre
   C Jefferson's massacre
   D Great Sioux massacre

<u>**American Civil War 2 (average)**</u>

Q1 What was the name of General Winfield Scott's plan to bring a swift end to the American Civil War?

Q2 Albert Sidney Johnston was killed in which battle?

Q3 What was the name of the theatre where Abraham Lincoln was assassinated?

Q4 Who commanded the Union Cavalry Corps at the Battle of Gettysburg?

Q5 Who is most commonly credited with the composition of the song *Dixie*?

Q6 At which courthouse did Robert E Lee surrender to Ulysses Grant?

Q7 The 1860 Democratic National Convention was held in which city?

Q8 Camp Douglas was located near which city?

Q9 The Battle of Hampton Roads marked what meeting in combat for the first time?

Q10 What was widely regarded as the most significant theatre in the American Civil War?

<u>**American Civil War 3 (expert)**</u>

Q1 Who was the first known casualty of the Civil War?

Q2 Who was the last surviving witness of Abraham Lincoln's assassination (died 1956)?

Q3 The Liberty Arsenal was located in which state?

Q4 Rioting broke out in which city on 19th April 1861?

Q5 Which Swiss officer was executed for war crimes at the end of the American Civil War?

Q6 Who ran against Abraham Lincoln in the 1864 presidential election?

Q7 What was the first steam-powered ironclad warship built by the Confederate States?

Q8 Who led Union forces in the Atlanta Campaign?

Q9 What was the name of the primary military force of the Confederate States of America in the Eastern Theatre of the American Civil War?

Q10 What was the real name of the Confederate commander the 'Gray Ghost'?

Franco-Prussian War (average)

Q1 Which territories did France lose in the Franco-Prussian War?

Q2 The Second French Empire became what after the Franco-Prussian War?

Q3 Which country was formed during the Franco-Prussian War?

Q4 Who was captured at the Battle of Sedan?

Q5 Who served as the President of the Government of National Defence?

Q6 Which peace treaty was signed at the end of the Franco-Prussian War?

Q7 Who was King of Prussia during the Franco-Prussian War?

Q8 In what year did Paris fall to the Prussians?

Q9 Which political figure instigated the Franco-Prussian War?

Q10 What position did Helmuth von Moltke the Elder hold in the Prussian military?

<u>**First World War 1 (easy)**</u>

Q1 The Zimmermann Telegram (1917) proposed an alliance between which two countries?

    A USA and Mexico
    B USA and Britain
    C Germany and France
    D Germany and Mexico

Q2 Which major ocean liner was sunk by a German U-boat on 7 May 1915?

    A RMS *Lusitania*
    B RMS *Titanic*
    C RMS *Olympic*
    D RMS *Mauretania*

Q3 What was the nationality of Archduke Franz Ferdinand's assassin, Gavrilo Princip?

    A Austrian
    B Bulgarian
    C Russian
    D Serbian

Q4 Stormtroopers were specialist soldiers in which army?

    A Austro-Hungarian
    B British
    C French
    D German

Q5 The Brusilov Offensive, one of the most lethal offensives in history, was launched by which country?

    A Russia
    B Germany
    C Austria-Hungary
    D USA

Q6 In what year did the USA enter the First World War?

A 1914
B 1916
C 1917
D 1918

Q7 What was the name of the peace treaty that brought the First World War to an end?

A Treaty of Paris
B Treaty of Vannes
C Treaty of Versailles
D Treaty of Berlin

Q8 What was the First World War known as?

A The patriot's war
B The war of empires
C The war of Germanisation
D The war to end all wars

Q9 How many great monarchies fell as a result of the First World War?

A 1
B 3
C 5
D 8

Q10 Which sea was the Battle of Jutland fought in?

A North Sea
B Red Sea
C Mediterranean Sea
D Black Sea

<u>**First World War 2 (average)**</u>

Q1 Which countries were members of the Triple Alliance upon the outbreak of World War One?

Q2 Who devised the Schlieffen Plan?

Q3 During the First World War what did George V change the House of Saxe-Coburg and Gotha's name to?

Q4 Horatio Herbert Kitchener held what rank in the British Army?

Q5 Who was President of the USA when it entered the First World War?

Q6 In which battle did Germany use poison gas in large quantities for the first time?

Q7 Which side in the First World War did Japan support?

Q8 Which two countries won the First Battle of the Marne?

Q9 Who was Chief of the German General Staff during the second half of the First World War?

Q10 John Jellicoe was an officer in which of the United Kingdom's armed forces?

<u>**First World War 3 (expert)**</u>

Q1 Which member of the Triple Alliance ultimately fought alongside the rival Triple Entente?

Q2 What was the nationality of spy Mata Hari?

Q3 Who was commander of the British Expeditionary Force?

Q4 Which 1839 treaty played a major role in the United Kingdom's entry into the First World War?

Q5 Which battle began the Hundred Days Offensive?

Q6 The Hindenburg Line was built during the winter of which years?

Q7 Which fleets fought each other at the Battle of Jutland?

Q8 What Royal Navy policy was a key cause of Germany resorting to unrestricted submarine warfare?

Q9 Little Willie was a type of what?

Q10 Which Russian general committed suicide after the Battle of Tannenberg?

Q1 Who did the Reds fight in the Russian Civil War?

Q2 Who was Russia's internationally recognised head of state between 1918 and 1920?

Q3 The Wrangel's Fleet refers to the last remnant of what?

Q4 Which five parts of the Russian Empire became sovereign states during the Russian Civil War?

Q5 What was the first Soviet police force called?

Q6 In what year was the Treaty of Brest-Litovsk signed?

Q7 The Polar Bear Expedition refers to foreign intervention in the Russian Civil War by what country?

Q8 Who wrote the *April Theses*?

Q9 Who were responsible for the Red Terror?

Q10 The Committee of Members of the Constituent Assembly was based in what city?

Spanish Civil War (average)

Q1 The Spanish Civil War took place in what years?

Q2 Who ruled over Spain as a military dictator after his victory in the Spanish Civil War?

Q3 In what year did the Bombing of Guernica occur?

Q4 The Spanish Civil War was fought between which two factions?

Q5 Who was the last President of the Second Spanish Republic?

Q6 What policy did the United Kingdom and France pursue in the Spanish Civil War?

Q7 Which two fascist regimes were heavily involved in the Spanish Civil War?

Q8 What two kinds of salute were used during the Spanish Civil War?

Q9 What name was given to the spate of political assassinations that occurred in Spain between 1936 and 1945?

Q10 Which military campaign was launched after the Battle of Teruel?

<u>**Second World War 1 (easy)**</u>

Q1 The Holocaust was a genocide primarily targeted at which group?

    A Catholics
    B Jews
    C Muslims
    D Fascists

Q2 Who became Chancellor of Germany for 2 days after the death of Hitler?

    A Reinhard Heydrich
    B Hermann Göring
    C Joseph Goebbels
    D Heinrich Himmler

Q3 Wernher von Braun played a major role in the development of which missile?

    A V-1
    B V-2
    C Exocet
    D BrahMos

Q4 What country was Adolf Hitler born in?

    A Austria
    B Czech Republic
    C Germany
    D Russia

Q5 The military tribunals held by the Allied forces under international law after World War Two were centred on which city?

    A Berlin
    B Paris
    C Nuremburg
    D Geneva

Q6 Which famous aircraft was designed by Reginald Mitchell?

A Lancaster
B Hurricane
C Spitfire
D Mosquito

Q7 In which theatre of the Second World War did the Brazilian Expeditionary Force fight?

A European Theatre
B Mediterranean and Middle East Theatre
C American Theatre
D South-East Asian Theatre

Q8 Which German general was known as the Desert Fox?

A Paul von Hindenburg
B Paul von Lettow-Vorbeck
C Erwin Rommel
D Reinhard Scheer

Q9 In what year was Dachau concentration camp established?

A 1933
B 1937
C 1942
D 1945

Q10 What type of plane dropped the 2 atomic bombs on Japan?

A Boeing B-29 Superfortress
B Handley Page Halifax
C Consolidated B-24 Liberator
D Consolidated B-32 Dominator

<u>**Second World War 2 (average)**</u>

Q1 What was the first air raid by the United States Air Force to strike the Japanese Home Islands called?

Q2 What does Blitzkrieg mean in English?

Q3 What was the name of the non-aggression pact signed between Germany and the Soviet Union in 1939?

Q4 On which peninsula was the Yalta Conference held?

Q5 On what date did the Normandy landings take place?

Q6 What was the last European city to be liberated from Nazi occupation?

Q7 What group of islands did the Japanese attack the day after Pearl Harbour?

Q8 Who did Hitler marry shortly before committing suicide?

Q9 The Luftwaffe refers to which branch of the German armed forces?

Q10 What was the first naval battle of the Second World War?

Second World War 3 (expert)

Q1 What did Hitler plan on renaming Berlin?

Q2 Exercise Tiger was a rehearsal for what?

Q3 What was the largest battle involving tanks in the Second World War?

Q4 The Second Battle of El Alamein was part of which military campaign?

Q5 At what battle was the USS *Lexington* sunk?

Q6 Tamon Yamaguchi died during which naval battle?

Q7 Which aircraft carrier was nicknamed the Big E?

Q8 The 1945 UK general election marked the first time the Conservative Party lost the popular vote since which election?

Q9 Who devised the Marshall Plan?

Q10 What nickname was Joseph Stalin given in Western propaganda during the Second World War?

Q1 Who was the first leader of North Korea?

Q2 The Korean Armistice Agreement was signed in what year?

Q3 What position did Syngman Rhee hold?

Q4 The Battle of Pusan Perimeter was fought between North Korea and which organisation?

Q5 The Military Demarcation Line runs near which circle of latitude?

Q6 Which two major powers supported North Korea?

Q7 Which country controlled Korea before 1945?

Q8 The South Korean Army destroyed which bridge on 28th June 1950?

Q9 An amphibious invasion was launched from which sea at the Battle of Inchon?

Q10 Edward Almond commanded which corps of the United States Army?

<u>**Vietnam War 1 (easy)**</u>

Q1 What was Operation Rolling Thunder?

    A Military offensive into North Vietnam
    B Entry of the United States Army into Vietnam
    C Aerial bombardment campaign
    D Assassination attempt on Ho Chi Minh

Q2 How many United States presidents were involved in the Vietnam War?

    A 2
    B 3
    C 4
    D 5

Q3 Which US Navy ship was involved in the Gulf of Tonkin incident?

    A *USS Massachusetts*
    B USS *Enterprise*
    C USS *Maine*
    D USS *Maddox*

Q4 What is Gary Rader well-known for doing?

    A Killing Ngo Dinh Diem
    B Firing the first shot in the Vietnam War
    C Burning his draft card
    D Escaping a prisoner of war camp

Q5 Besides from North and South Vietnam, where else were battles fought during the Vietnam War?

    A North Korea
    B China
    C Thailand
    D Laos

Q6 Which US President pursued a policy of Vietnamization?

    A Dwight Eisenhower
    B John F Kennedy
    C Lyndon B Johnson
    D Richard Nixon

Q7 What was a *punji*?

    A Hat
    B Booby trap
    C Knife
    D Internment camp

Q8 What were the refugees who fled South Vietnam at the end of the Vietnam War called?

    A The Persecuted
    B Capitalists
    C Boat people
    D Pioneers

Q9 What was the capital of North Vietnam?

    A Ho Chi Minh City
    B Da Nang
    C Hanoi
    D Hue

Q10 Which US President announced the formal normalization of diplomatic relations between the USA and Vietnam in 1995?

    A Ronald Reagan
    B George H W Bush
    C Bill Clinton
    D George W Bush

<u>**Vietnam War 2 (average)**</u>

Q1 Who was the United States Secretary of Defence between 1961 and 1968?

Q2 In what year did the Tet Offensive take place?

Q3 The Gulf of Tonkin Resolution was passed by which legislature?

Q4 Which chemical weapon was used during Operation Ranch Hand?

Q5 Which trail famously provided support to the Việt Cộng?

Q6 What other name was the Việt Cộng known by?

Q7 What theory played a key role in American intervention in Vietnam?

Q8 What event marked the end of the Vietnam War?

Q9 What was Saigon renamed after the Vietnam War?

Q10 Which future US Senator for Arizona was a prisoner of war during the Vietnam War?

<u>**Vietnam War 3 (expert)**</u>

Q1 In what year did the My Lai Massacre occur?

Q2 What did American prisoners of war call Hỏa Lò Prison?

Q3 Operation Pocket Money took place in what year?

Q4 The Battle of Hamburger Hill was fought during which operation?

Q5 Because no official declaration of war was made, how did the United States refer to its military intervention in Vietnam?

Q6 What was the name of the first turbine-powered helicopter produced for the United States military?

Q7 The Case–Church Amendment was effective from what year?

Q8 Phan Thi Kim Phuc appears in a well-known photograph taken by who?

Q9 Members of the Ohio National Guard shot unarmed students at which university in 1970?

Q10 Which film director won numerous medals for bravery in the Vietnam War?

Ancient World

Q1 The *ankh* is a hieroglyphic symbol representing what?

> **A** Life
> **B** Death
> **C** Rebirth
> **D** The Pharaoh

Q2 What animal is said to have killed Cleopatra?

> **A** Lion
> **B** Cobra
> **C** Scorpion
> **D** Crocodile

Q3 The Karnak Temple Complex is located near which present-day Egyptian city?

> **A** Cairo
> **B** Luxor
> **C** Aswan
> **D** Alexandria

Q4 In which museum can the Rosetta Stone be found?

> **A** Smithsonian Institution
> **B** Louvre Museum
> **C** The Museum of Egyptian Antiquities
> **D** British Museum

Q5 Which archaeologist discovered Tutankhamun's tomb in 1922?

> **A** Adolf Erman
> **B** Fernand Bisson de la Roque
> **C** Howard Carter
> **D** Zahi Hawass

Q6 Which Ramesses was known as 'the Great'?

    A Ramesses I
    B Ramesses II
    C Ramesses III
    D Ramesses IV

Q7 Who was the sun god in Ancient Egyptian mythology?

    A Isis
    B Seth
    C Ra
    D Anubis

Q8 Who is widely regarded as being the founder of the First Dynasty?

    A Ramesses the Great
    B Menes
    C Tutankhamun
    D Ptolemy I

Q9 The Narmer Palette can be roughly dated to which century?

    A 40th century BC
    B 31st century BC
    C 19th century BC
    D 3rd century BC

Q10 The arrival of the Hyksos initiated which period of Ancient Egyptian history?

    A Early Dynastic Period
    B Old Kingdom
    C Middle Kingdom
    D Second Intermediate Period

Ancient Egypt 2 (average)

Q1 What two regions was Ancient Egypt divided into?

Q2 Which New Kingdom pharaoh is believed to have been the first to be buried in the Valley of the Kings?

Q3 Who did the Egyptians fight at the Battle of Kadesh?

Q4 In Egyptian mythology, what is the *Duat*?

Q5 Which pharaoh's reign does the Rosetta Stone originate from?

Q6 Who succeeded Tutankhamun as pharaoh?

Q7 Which is further north: Upper Egypt or Lower Egypt?

Q8 Ancient Egyptian obelisks were re-erected in which three major Western cities during the nineteenth century?

Q9 What is the first Ancient Egyptian pyramid called?

Q10 Luxor Temple is located on which bank of the River Nile?

<u>**Ancient Egypt 3 (expert)**</u>

Q1 Who was the architect of the first tomb built in the Valley of the Kings?

Q2 Which four organs were kept in canopic jars?

Q3 What was Tutankhamun's throne name?

Q4 Which archaeologist discovered the Merneptah Stele in 1896?

Q5 What was Tutankhamun's tomb named by archaeologists?

Q6 Which Egyptologist developed sequence dating?

Q7 Which Egyptian priest authored the *Aegyptiaca* (History of Egypt)?

Q8 What is the Old Kingdom's oldest known corpus of religious texts?

Q9 Which pharaoh organised the first recorded expedition to the Land of Punt?

Q10 Psamtik III was defeated by which empire at the Battle of Pelusium?

<u>Ancient Greece 1 (easy)</u>

Q1 Alexander the Great was king of what?

    A Cyprus
    B Sparta
    C Macedonia
    D Athens

Q2 Pericles was a prominent statesman in which city?

    A Argos
    B Athens
    C Corinth
    D Thessaloniki

Q3 What was an Asclepeion?

    A Healing temple
    B Barracks
    C Palace
    D Arena

Q4 What is the Philopappos Monument?

    A Church
    B Mausoleum
    C Fountain
    D Palace

Q5 Who is said to have been the first King of Athens?

    A Erichthonius
    B Erechtheus
    C Cecrops I
    D Menestheus

Q6 The Battle of Corinth was fought between Corinth and which major power?

    A Mongol Empire
    B Achaemenid Empire
    C Akkadian Empire
    D Roman Republic

Q7 What was Lysippos's occupation?

    A Military commander
    B Sculptor
    C Navigator
    D Mathematician

Q8 Mamertines were mercenaries who originated from which present-day country?

    A Greece
    B Germany
    C Italy
    D Turkey

Q9 What metal was a Corinthian helmet made from?

    A Gold
    B Bronze
    C Steel
    D Iron

Q10 A *metic* was a foreign resident of which Greek city state?

    A Thebes
    B Eretria
    C Athens
    D Corinth

<u>Ancient Greece 2 (average)</u>

Q1 What is the earliest alphabet known for the Greek language?

Q2 In Greek mythology, which side did Penthesilea fight on in the Trojan War?

Q3 What was the prize for the winner of the ancient Olympic Games?

Q4 The Delian League, founded in 478 BC, was created for what purpose?

Q5 The Academy in Athens was founded by which philosopher?

Q6 Solon is often credited with laying the foundations of what kind of democracy?

Q7 Gortyn is an archaeological site on which island?

Q8 The *ephors* were leaders of which Ancient Greek city state?

Q9 What are the Twelve Olympians?

Q10 Pederasty involved a socially acceptable romantic relationship between an adult and a teenager of what gender?

<u>**Ancient Greece 3 (expert)**</u>

Q1 Which archaeologist unearthed the Palace of Knossos on Crete?

Q2 Where were the Pythian Games held?

Q3 The Peloponnesian War was fought between which two leagues?

Q4 The term 'pyrrhic victory' is named after King Pyrrhus of Epirus, whose army suffered irreplaceable casualties in defeating the Romans at which two battles?

Q5 What was the occupation of Euclid of Alexandria?

Q6 Which Greek civilisation preceded the Greek Dark Ages?

Q7 The Lelantine War was fought between which two city states?

Q8 What was the name of the high priestess of the Temple of Apollo at Delphi?

Q9 Which king played a key role in the formation of the Ancient Macedonian army?

Q10 What was the Antikythera mechanism?

<u>Ancient Rome 1 (easy)</u>

Q1 Who was the first emperor of the Roman Empire?

    A Augustus
    B Caesar
    C Nero
    D Mark Antony

Q2 Which of the following was a currency of Ancient Rome?

    A Drachma
    B Shekel
    C Sesterce
    D Pound

Q3 Which emperor converted the Roman Empire to Christianity in 313?

    A Caligula
    B Hadrian
    C Tiberius
    D Constantine

Q4 Which river did Julius Caesar famously cross, sparking the Great Roman Civil War?

    A Tiber
    B Rubicon
    C Po
    D Arno

Q5 Who sacked Rome in 410AD?

    A Visigoths
    B Huns
    C Vandals
    D Franks

Q6 What was a *scutum*?

    A Crossbow
    B Sword
    C Shield
    D Helmet

Q7 'Veni, vidi, vici' is a phrase popularly attributed to who?

    A Cicero
    B Trajan
    C Julius Caesar
    D Commodus

Q8 How many continents did the Roman Empire have territories in?

    A 1
    B 2
    C 3
    D 4

Q9 The Roman–Persian Wars endured for just under how many centuries?

    A 2
    B 3
    C 5
    D 7

Q10 What was the Circus Maximus used for?

    A Chariot racing
    B Army training
    C Coronations
    D Acrobatics

<u>**Ancient Rome 2 (average)**</u>

Q1 Which brothers are said to have founded Rome?

Q2 The emperor Elagabalus originated from which present-day country?

Q3 Pompeii and which other town were the principal victims of the 79 AD eruption of Mount Vesuvius?

Q4 Who adopted Nero before he became emperor?

Q5 The construction of the Coliseum began during the reign of which emperor?

Q6 The Roman Empire reached its greatest territorial extent under which emperor?

Q7 In which naval battle did Rome decisively defeat the forces of Antony and Cleopatra?

Q8 Which gladiator led a two-year slave revolt against the Romans?

Q9 Zeno of Citium founded what school of philosophy?

Q10 What acronym refers to the government of the Roman Republic?

<u>**Ancient Rome 3 (expert)**</u>

Q1 The largest standing Roman monument in northern Europe, the Porta Nigra, is located in which city?

Q2 Aquae Sulis was the Roman name for which English city?

Q3 Pliny the Elder died during which disaster?

Q4 What three periods cover the history of Ancient Rome?

Q5 Which Roman Emperors are commonly known as the Five Good Emperors?

Q6 What city became capital of the Western Roman Empire in 402 AD?

Q7 Who did the Romans fight at the Battle of the Allia?

Q8 Fabian strategy was a military strategy which aimed to avoid what?

Q9 Cato the Elder was well-known for his opposition to the spread of which culture?

Q10 The Edict of Milan was an agreement between Constantine the Great and who else?

Pre-Columbian Americas

Q1 Cahokia is located near which present-day city?

    A Amarillo, Texas
    B St Louis, Missouri
    C Atlanta, Georgia
    D Santa Fe, New Mexico

Q2 Pontiac's War was fought between a loose confederation of Native American tribes and which country?

    A USA
    B France
    C United Kingdom
    D Spain

Q3 Through which strait are Native American peoples believed to have entered the Americas?

    A Washington Strait
    B Bering Strait
    C Russia-Alaska Strait
    D Tecumseh Strait

Q4 Powhatan was native to which present-day US state?

    A Florida
    B Connecticut
    C Ohio
    D Virginia

Q5 Plains Indians were heavily reliant on what animal for survival?

    A Wolf
    B Cow
    C Buffalo
    D Turkey

Q6 What is Watson Brake?

A Archaeological site
B Reservation
C Mass burial
D Mythological city

Q7 The Trail of Tears involved the forced relocation of Native American peoples west of which river?

A Rio Grande
B Ohio River
C Mississippi River
D Canadian River

Q8 The Seminole people were originally from which US state?

A Oklahoma
B Arkansas
C Georgia
D Florida

Q9 The 'Eastern Woodlands' refers to a cultural area extending roughly from the Atlantic Ocean to where?

A Great Plains
B Rocky Mountains
C Cumberland Mountains
D Mississippi River

Q10 Head-Smashed-In Buffalo Jump is located in which Canadian province?

A Alberta
B Saskatchewan
C Yukon
D Nova Scotia

<u>**North America 2 (average)**</u>

Q1 Which Lemhi Shoshone woman is associated with the Lewis and Clark Expedition?

Q2 What name is given by North American archaeologists to the period 8000 to 1000 BC?

Q3 By what name are the first people to enter the Americas referred to?

Q4 Which US state is nicknamed 'Native America'?

Q5 Poverty Point culture is associated with the construction of what?

Q6 What is the largest earthwork in the Americas called?

Q7 The Natchez revolt involved an attack against colonists from which country?

Q8 What does mixed-blood refer to?

Q9 In what battle was Tecumseh killed?

Q10 Which part of the human body did numerous Native American tribes take from their enemies?

<u>**North America 3 (expert)**</u>

Q1 Little Turtle was a war chief of which Native American people?

Q2 The Hopewell tradition existed during which period of North American history?

Q3 Cahokia is associated with which Native American civilisation?

Q4 The term 'Five Civilised Tribes' refers to which five Native American nations?

Q5 Which Native American people did Christopher Columbus first encounter?

Q6 Anzick-1 (the name given to the remains of male infant discovered in Montana) is associated with which culture?

Q7 Xá:ytem is an indigenous archaeological site in which Canadian province?

Q8 What name did Norse explorers use to refer to the people they encountered in North America and Greenland?

Q9 What does the term 'Eskimo' mean?

Q10 The Ahwahnechee lived in which valley?

<u>**Maya 1 (easy)**</u>

Q1 Diego de Landa is infamous for burning Mayan what?

A Towns
B Civilians
C Codices
D Crops

Q2 El Castillo step-pyramid can be found at which archaeological site?

A Coba
B Copán
C Ek' Balam
D Chichen Itza

Q3 The earliest inscriptions of Maya script have been dated to what century?

A 10th century BC
B 3rd century BC
C 5th century AD
D 11th century AD

Q4 Maya stelae were monuments made out of what?

A Stone
B Wood
C Obsidian
D Bones

Q5 Sacrifice victims were sometimes painted what colour?

A Blue
B Red
C Orange
D Black

Q6 *Amate* was a type of what?

A Shoe
B Arrow
C Canoe
D Paper

Q7 In what year did Martín de Ursúa defeat the last significant Maya stronghold, Nojpetén?

A 1498
B 1510
C 1550
D 1697

Q8 Kinich Ahau was the Maya god of what?

A Wind
B Fertility
C Sun
D War

Q9 A roof comb topped what?

A Headdress
B Pyramid
C Altar
D Marketplace

Q10 What was Xibalba in K'iche' Maya mythology?

A Lost city
B Ancestral homeland
C Underworld
D Realm of the gods

<u>**Maya 2 (average)**</u>

Q1 What was the Mayan name for the Mesoamerican god Quetzalcoatl?

Q2 Nakbe is an archaeological site located in what country?

Q3 Chak Tok Ich'aak I was an *ajaw* of what Maya city?

Q4 Did the Mayans use a matrilineal or patrilineal kinship system?

Q5 The Triadic pyramid was an innovation of which period of Mayan history?

Q6 Chichen Itza shares considerable similarities with which Toltec city?

Q7 What is the volcanic glass called that was commonly used in the blades of Maya weapons?

Q8 The Maya civilisation stretched from southern Mexico to which present-day country?

Q9 What were dogs raised for by the Maya?

Q10 As well as for food, what else were cacao beans used for by the Maya?

<u>**Maya 3 (expert)**</u>

Q1 The Mayan numeral system was based on what number?

Q2 Nojpetén was the capital city of which kingdom?

Q3 What is the modern version of the Mesoamerican ballgame called?

Q4 Who discovered Calakmul from the air?

Q5 Who is believed to have reigned longer than any other Mesoamerican ruler?

Q6 Which three codices are confirmed to have been produced in Pre-Columbian times?

Q7 What were the names of the Maya Hero Twins?

Q8 *Popol Vuh* is a cultural narrative that recounts the mythology and history of which people?

Q9 What physical feature did the Maya consider to be beautiful?

Q10 What period of Maya history began in the 10th century AD?

<u>**Aztec 1 (easy)**</u>

Q1 The capital of the Aztec Empire, Tenochtitlan, was based on the site of which present-day city?

    A Mexico City
    B Monterrey
    C Cancún
    D Mérida

Q2 In Aztec mythology, what world were they in?

    A First
    B Second
    C Fourth
    D Fifth

Q3 Who was the first *tlatoani* of Tenochtitlan?

    A Moctezuma I
    B Acamapichtli
    C Chimalpopoca
    D Itzcoatl

Q4 What was an *altepetl*?

    A Mass burial
    B Temple
    C Market
    D City state

Q5 What was the name of the ritual war fought intermittently between the Aztecs and their enemies from the mid-15th century until the arrival of the Spanish Conquistadores?

    A Bloody Wars
    B Wars of Unification
    C Flower Wars
    D Aztec Wars

Q6 What title did Tlacaelel most notably hold?

    A *Tlatoani*
    B *Tlacochcalcatl*
    C *Tlacateccatl*
    D *Tlamemeh*

Q7 What were *pochteca*?

    A Warriors
    B Advisors
    C Long-distance merchants
    D Slaves

Q8 What type of laws prohibited commoners from wearing adornments such as lip plugs, gold armbands and cotton cloaks?

    A Oppressive laws
    B Hierarchy laws
    C Sumptuary laws
    D Regal laws

Q9 Who was *tlatoani* of Texcoco between1429 and 1472?

    A Tayatzin
    B Itzcoatl
    C Tezozomoc
    D Nezahualcoyotl

Q10 What was the main temple in Tenochtitlan called?

    A Great Pyramid
    B Templo Mayor
    C Temple of Quetzalcoatl
    D Moctezuma's Wonder

<u>**Aztec 2 (average)**</u>

Q1 The Aztec Empire was known by what other name?

Q2 The Aztec sun stone was rediscovered during repairs on what building?

Q3 *The Florentine Codex* is an ethnographic research study carried out by which Franciscan friar?

Q4 Which *altepetl* were the Aztecs initially subjects of when they arrived in the Valley of Mexico?

Q5 What was the name of Tenochtitlan's sister city?

Q6 During the Spanish siege of Tenochtitlan, what disease did many of the Aztec capital's inhabitants die from?

Q7 Tzintzuntzan was the ceremonial centre of which state?

Q8 Who was the Aztec god of rain?

Q9 In Aztec mythology, how many caves were there at Chicomoztoc?

Q10 Tenochtitlan was founded where an eagle with a snake in its beak landed on what kind of plant?

<u>**Aztec 3 (expert)**</u>

Q1 What did the Aztecs create on shallow lake beds to grow crops on?

Q2 Moquihuix was *tlatoani* of which *altepetl*?

Q3 The Massacre in the Great Temple occurred while a festival was being held in honour of which god?

Q4 Who was the last Aztec *tlatoani* before Tenochtitlan fell to the Spanish?

Q5 What was *patolli*?

Q6 In Aztec mythology, what is the name of the ancestral home of the Mexica people?

Q7 What does the name Chimalpopoca mean?

Q8 What is a *tzompantli* better known as?

Q9 In Aztec society an *altepetl* was divided into a number of what?

Q10 What social class were *tlahcotin* a part of?

<u>**Inca 1 (easy)**</u>

Q1 What was the name of the Inca sun god?

    A Pachamama
    B Mama Quilla
    C Inti
    D Viracocha

Q2 Who was the last *Sapa Inca* of the Inca Empire?

    A Huáscar
    B Atahualpa
    C Huayna Capac
    D Manco Cápac

Q3 What was the capital of the Inca Empire?

    A Cuzco
    B Machu Picchu
    C Ollantaytambo
    D Lima

Q4 Who led the conquest of the Inca Empire?

    A Hernán Cortés
    B Hernando de Soto
    C Pánfilo de Narváez
    D Francisco Pizarro

Q5 How many provinces was the Inca Empire composed of?

    A 1
    B 4
    C 10
    D 12

Q6 What is Quechua?

    A First month of the Inca year
    B An administrative region
    C Noble title
    D Language family

Q7 In what century was the Chimor-Inca War fought?

    A 11th century
    B 13th century
    C 15th century
    D 16th century

Q8 In what year was the Battle of Puná fought?

    A 1505
    B 1518
    C 1531
    D 1599

Q9 The Children of Llullaillaco refers to how many Inca child mummies?

    A 2
    B 3
    C 10
    D 60

Q10 *Qhapaq hucha* involved the sacrifice of what?

    A Children
    B Cattle
    C Slaves
    D Captured warriors

<u>**Inca 2 (average)**</u>

Q1 The Sacred Valley of the Incas is known by what other name?

Q2 Which American explorer made public the existence of Machu Picchu?

Q3 What was a *suyu*?

Q4 Ninan Cuyochi was the eldest son of which *Sapa Inca*?

Q5 What were the Willaq Umu?

Q6 Which religious ceremony is held in honour of the Inca sun god?

Q7 What famous geoglyphs are located in the Nazca Desert?

Q8 What was Sacsayhuamán?

Q9 The Ransom Room is located in which city?

Q10 Manco Inca Yupanqui founded which state?

<u>**Inca 3 (expert)**</u>

Q1 What is Intihuatana?

Q2 What were objects called – both natural and manmade – that were revered by the Incas for spiritual reasons?

Q3 Who was the Inca earth goddess?

Q4 Which two large empires existed in South America before 1100?

Q5 The Inca Civil War was fought between which two brothers?

Q6 What was *mit'a*?

Q7 Sinchiruca commanded Inca forces which were defeated at which three-day battle?

Q8 What was a *qiru*?

Q9 In what year was Túpac Amaru executed?

Q10 What was the capital city of the Neo-Inca State?

English Monarchs

<u>**William I (easy)**</u>

Q1 Besides from 'the Conqueror', what other nickname did William I have?

  A The Brave
  B The Bastard
  C The Cruel
  D The Cunning

Q2 How many of William I's sons went on to become King of England?

  A 0
  B 1
  C 2
  D 3

Q3 In which battle did William beat the King of England, Harold Godwinson?

  A Battle of Hastings
  B Battle of Stamford Bridge
  C Battle of Edington
  D Battle of Badon

Q4 In which town did William I die?

  A Bayeux
  B London
  C Rouen
  D York

Q5 After the Norman Conquest, what did William I change the language of government in England to?

  A English
  B French
  C Breton
  D Basque

Q6 After being crowned King of England, how long was it before William I returned to Normandy?

    A 3 months
    B 1 year
    C 5 years
    D Never

Q7 How did William I primarily consolidate his conquest?

    A Military occupation
    B Built castles
    C Killed rival claimants
    D Starved the population

Q8 Which of the following was William I not responsible for?

    A Tower of London
    B Reconstruction of Durham Cathedral
    C Domesday Book
    D Church of England

Q9 Where was William I crowned King of England?

    A York Minster
    B St Paul's Cathedral
    C Westminster Abbey
    D Reims Cathedral

Q10 Who did William I fight against at the siege and battle of Gerberoy in the winter of 1078-79?

    A Robert Curthose
    B William Rufus
    C Harold Godwinson
    D Odo of Bayeux

William I (average)

Q1 What day of the year was William I crowned King of England?

Q2 Who was William I's wife?

Q3 Who became Duke of Normandy after William I's death?

Q4 Who did William and the French king, Henry I, defeat at the Battle of Varaville?

Q5 In what year was the Domesday Book completed?

Q6 Which abbey did William I have constructed as penance for the bloodshed at the Battle of Hastings?

Q7 How many volumes is the *Domesday Book* composed of?

Q8 Who did William I appoint as Archbishop of Canterbury in 1070?

Q9 Which area of Hampshire was proclaimed a royal forest by William I?

Q10 The injury that led to William I's death is said to have occurred while he was doing what?

William I (expert)

Q1 What relation was Edward the Confessor to William I?

Q2 Who was William I's mother, Herleva, married to?

Q3 Where did William I land in England, beginning the Norman Conquest?

Q4 The Harrying of the North occurred during the winter of which years?

Q5 Where was Hereward the Wake's base when leading his rebellion against Norman rulers?

Q6 In which treaty did Malcolm III of Scotland recognise William I as his feudal overlord?

Q7 In what year did William the Conqueror become Duke of Normandy?

Q8 How many days separated the Battle of Stamford Bridge and the Battle of Hastings?

Q9 William I's half-brother Odo held what two titles?

Q10 Approximately how long is the Bayeux Tapestry (in metres)?

<u>**William II (average)**</u>

Q1 In which forest did William II die in 1100?

Q2 Why was William II also called William Rufus?

Q3 How many children did William II have?

Q4 The 'Rufus Stone' claims to mark what?

Q5 Who led the Rebellion of 1088?

Q6 Who did William II appoint Archbishop of Canterbury in 1093?

Q7 In 1091 William II repulsed an invasion by which Scottish king?

Q8 William II's older brother, Robert Curthose, took part in which crusade?

Q9 The earliest reference to William II's death is in which chronicle?

Q10 Which cathedral was William II buried in?

<u>**Henry I (easy)**</u>

Q1 What was the name of the ship that sank in 1120, killing Henry I's son and heir William Adelin?

    A The *White Ship*
    B The *Black Ship*
    C *Queen Anne's Revenge*
    D HMS *Victory*

Q2 How many times did Henry I marry?

    A 0
    B 1
    C 2
    D 3

Q3 What was the name of the period of civil war that followed Henry I's death?

    A Wars of the Roses
    B English Civil War
    C Glorious Revolution
    D The Anarchy

Q4 How many brothers did Henry I have?

    A 0
    B 1
    C 3
    D 4

Q5 After his father's death, where did Henry I initially live?

    A England
    B France
    C Scotland
    D Normandy

Q6 During his coronation, Henry I promised a return to the gentler customs of which former English king?

A William I
B Alfred the Great
C Edward the Confessor
D Edward the Martyr

Q7 The Charter of Liberties is known by what other name?

A The Coronation Charter
B The Great Charter
C The Royal Charter
D The People's Charter

Q8 Which royal house did Henry I belong to?

A Tudor
B Stuart
C Normandy
D Plantagenet

Q9 In what year did Henry I die?

A 1066
B 1100
C 1120
D 1135

Q10 What happened to Ranulf Flambard, Bishop of Durham on Henry I's rise to power?

A Imprisoned
B Executed
C Baptised
D Betrothed

<u>**Henry I (average)**</u>

Q1 In which duchy did Henry I die?

Q2 Which relative did Henry defeat at the Battle of Tinchebray?

Q3 What was the primary motivation behind Henry I's decision to marry Adeliza of Louvain in 1121?

Q4 How many years after the Norman Conquest was Henry I born?

Q5 Why wasn't Robert Curthose present to claim the throne of England when William II died?

Q6 What was the name of Henry I's first legitimate child?

Q7 Henry I had a dispute with which Archbishop of Canterbury in the early stages of his reign?

Q8 Who did Henry I betroth his eldest daughter to in 1108?

Q9 The Battle of Brémule was fought between Henry I and who?

Q10 According to the chronicler Henry of Huntingdon, eating too much what caused Henry I's death?

Henry I (expert)

Q1 Where was Henry I buried?

Q2 Who crowned Henry I king?

Q3 In what year was the Treaty of Alton signed?

Q4 In what year did Henry I replace his elder brother, Robert Curthose, as Duke of Normandy?

Q5 What did Henry I keep at Woodstock Palace?

Q6 The oldest surviving Pipe Roll dates from which year of Henry I's reign?

Q7 Who was the captain of the ship that sank in 1120, killing William Adelin?

Q8 William Adelin was married to the eldest daughter of which count?

Q9 William Rufus's chancellor, William Giffard, became Bishop of what on Henry I's rise to power?

Q10 What are the names of the two kings who ruled France during Henry I's reign?

<u>**Stephen and Matilda (easy)**</u>

Q1 What was the name of the civil war that took place during Stephen's reign?

    A Wars of the Roses
    B The Anarchy
    C English Civil War
    D Glorious Revolution

Q2 What relation was Henry I to Stephen?

    A Father
    B Brother
    C Cousin
    D Uncle

Q3 Matilda's second husband was the founder of which royal house?

    A Plantagenet
    B Tudor
    C Blois
    D Normandy

Q4 Who was captured at the Battle of Lincoln (1141)?

    A King Stephen
    B Empress Matilda
    C Henry II
    D Robert FitzRoy, Earl of Gloucester

Q5 How many children did Matilda have with her first husband?

    A 0
    B 1
    C 2
    D 5

Q6 Which crusade was fought during Stephen's reign?

    A First Crusade
    B Second Crusade
    C Third Crusade
    D Fourth Crusade

Q7 Matilda's mother, Matilda of Scotland, was originally christened with which name?

    A Elizabeth
    B Mary
    C Edith
    D Alexandra

Q8 Where is Matilda buried?

    A Tower of London
    B Windsor Castle
    C Westminster Abbey
    D Rouen Cathedral

Q9 In what year did Matilda cease to be Empress of the Holy Roman Empire?

    A 1125
    B 1135
    C 1154
    D 1167

Q10 Stephen and the future Henry II sealed the treaty that ended 18 years of civil war with a kiss of what?

    A Affection
    B Allegiance
    C Peace
    D Unity

Stephen and Matilda (average)

Q1 King Stephen is often referred to by what other name?

Q2 What was the name of Stephen's eldest son?

Q3 The Treaty of Wallingford ensured who would succeed Stephen as King of England?

Q4 Whose death caused a succession crisis?

Q5 The renowned historical source *Gesta Stephani* means roughly what in English?

Q6 Matilda died during which king's reign?

Q7 William of Ypres was a key military leader, loyal to who?

Q8 Stephen's wife was a member of which royal house?

Q9 Because she was never crowned Queen of England, what title has Matilda been given instead?

Q10 Matilda's half-brother Robert was Earl of what?

<u>**Stephen and Matilda (expert)**</u>

Q1 Between what years did the Anarchy occur?

Q2 Who led King Stephen's army at the Rout of Winchester?

Q3 Matilda fled from which castle, closely avoiding capture, in the winter of 1141-42?

Q4 In which abbey was Stephen buried?

Q5 Stephen's father was Count of what?

Q6 Where was Matilda crowned Holy Roman Empress?

Q7 Which Archbishop of Canterbury crowned Stephen King of England?

Q8 How many of Stephen's legitimate children lived into adulthood?

Q9 At what battle was Stephen's father killed?

Q10 Who was heir apparent to the English throne before Stephen agreed to adopt the future Henry II as his heir?

<u>Henry II (easy)</u>

Q1 How many of Henry II's sons went on to become King of England?

    A 1
    B 2
    C 3
    D 4

Q2 Henry II famously clashed with which Archbishop of Canterbury?

    A Thomas Becket
    B Hubert Walter
    C Simon Sudbury
    D Edmund of Abingdon

Q3 Henry II was the first person from which royal house to be King of England?

    A Normandy
    B Blois
    C Plantagenet
    D Orange-Nassau

Q4 Henry II was born in and died in which kingdom?

    A Kingdom of England
    B Kingdom of France
    C Kingdom of Castile
    D Kingdom of Bohemia

Q5 What colour hair is Henry II said to have had?

    A Brown
    B Black
    C Blond
    D Red

Q6 Which two languages did Henry II primarily speak?

    A English and French
    B English and Latin
    C French and Latin
    D French and Greek

Q7 In which cathedral did King Stephen announce the Treaty of Winchester?

    A St Paul's Cathedral
    B York Minster
    C Winchester Cathedral
    D Salisbury Cathedral

Q8 Where did Henry II invade in 1171?

    A Scotland
    B Ireland
    C Wales
    D France

Q9 What happened to Eleanor of Aquitaine between 1173 and 1189?

    A Returned to Aquitaine
    B Excommunicated
    C On pilgrimage
    D Imprisoned

Q10 Which holy city fell to Islamic forces in 1187?

    A Jerusalem
    B Rome
    C Nazareth
    D Bethlehem

<u>**Henry II (average)**</u>

Q1 What was the name of Henry II's wife?

Q2 Which son did Henry II discover had betrayed him just before he died?

Q3 Which treaty paved the way for Henry II being named King of England?

Q4 What was Henry II's nickname?

Q5 Who was King of France for the majority of Henry II's reign?

Q6 Henry II was the first ruler of which empire?

Q7 What did Henry II die from?

Q8 Ruaidrí Ua Conchobair was named what in 1166?

Q9 Which pope canonised Thomas Becket?

Q10 Henry II's father was Count of what?

<u>**Henry II (expert)**</u>

Q1 Where did Henry II die?

Q2 In what years did Henry the Young King serve as Junior King of England?

Q3 How many knights are said to have been involved in the murder of Thomas Becket?

Q4 Why was Adrian IV becoming pope in 1154 significant?

Q5 The Constitutions of Clarendon were passed by Henry II in what year?

Q6 Which Cambridge clerk almost had his arm chopped off when he tried to defend Thomas Becket?

Q7 Which king was captured at the Battle of Alnwick?

Q8 Which four close relatives of Henry II were involved in the Revolt of 1173–74?

Q9 *Tractatus de legibus et consuetudinibus regni Anglie* is the earliest treatise on what?

Q10 In which abbey is Henry II buried?

<u>**Richard I (easy)**</u>

Q1 Approximately how long did Richard I spend in England during his 10-year reign?

    A 6 months
    B 1 year
    C 3 years
    D 9 years

Q2 What was Richard I's nickname?

    A The Bold
    B The Patriot
    C The Lionheart
    D The Spendthrift

Q3 Which crusade was Richard I involved in?

    A First
    B Second
    C Third
    D Fourth

Q4 Richard I is often depicted as being the favourite of which relative?

    A His mother
    B His father
    C His eldest brother
    D His youngest sister

Q5 The Massacre of Ayyadieh occurred after the fall of which city?

    A Acre
    B Jerusalem
    C Damascus
    D Constantinople

Q6 In what year did Richard I become Duke of Normandy?

    A 1175
    B 1180
    C 1189
    D Never

Q7 In which kingdom did the Archbishop Canterbury, Baldwin of Forde, die?

    A Kingdom of England
    B Kingdom of France
    C Kingdom of Castile
    D Kingdom of Jerusalem

Q8 In 1190 a major massacre of Jews occurred in which city?

    A Winchester
    B Salisbury
    C Norwich
    D York

Q9 Richard I fought in the Battle of Arsuf against who?

    A Philip II of France
    B John of England
    C Baldwin V of Jerusalem
    D Saladin

Q10 The Knights Templar's allegiance was to which ruler?

    A King of England
    B King of France
    C King of Jerusalem
    D The Pope

Richard I (average)

Q1 In which duchy did Richard I die?

Q2 Who was Richard I's wife?

Q3 Which French king did Richard I go on crusade with?

Q4 Who was Richard I's main opponent whilst on crusade?

Q5 On Richard I's accession to the throne of England what position did William de Longchamp acquire?

Q6 Richard I and his brothers frequently rebelled against who?

Q7 Which group were the victims of serious prejudice during Richard I's reign?

Q8 On what island did Richard I of England and Philip II of France arrive on in September 1190?

Q9 In which city was Richard I's heart buried?

Q10 Richard I was killed with what weapon?

<u>**Richard I (expert)**</u>

Q1 In which abbey is Richard I buried?

Q2 After being captured by Leopold V, Duke of Austria, what castle was Richard I held in?

Q3 Who was Richard I's wet nurse?

Q4 The *Itinerarium Regis Ricardi* is a Latin prose narrative of what?

Q5 The scholar Jacob of Orléans was killed in London during what?

Q6 The Saladin tithe was raised in response to what?

Q7 What was the proper title of the Sheriff of Nottingham during Richard I's reign?

Q8 Who was designated heir to the throne of England in 1190?

Q9 Isaac Komnenos ruled which island before Richard I invaded it in 1191?

Q10 Richard I was married in which city?

<u>**John (easy)**</u>

Q1 What does Magna Carta mean in English?

    A Great Charter
    B Great Change
    C Great Constitution
    D Great Crimes

Q2 What was King John's nickname?

    A The Fearless
    B The Foolish
    C Lackland
    D The Cruel

Q3 King John was the youngest son of which King of England?

    A William II
    B Henry I
    C Henry II
    D Richard I

Q4 Which pope excommunicated King John in 1209?

    A Innocent III
    B Urban II
    C Gregory I
    D Benedict V

Q5 How many times did King John marry?

    A 0
    B 1
    C 2
    D 3

Q6 What did King John die from?

    A Wounds in battle
    B Dysentery
    C Heart attack
    D Liver failure

Q7 Who was King of Scotland for the majority of King John's reign?

    A Alexander II
    B Alexander III
    C James IV
    D William the Lion

Q8 Where was the Magna Carta agreed?

    A Smithfield
    B Runneymede
    C Tower of London
    D Nottingham Castle

Q9 Who became Archbishop of Canterbury in 1207?

    A Thomas Becket
    B Walter d'Eynsham
    C Ralph Neville
    D Stephen Langton

Q10 Which war resulted from King John's refusal to abide by the Magna Carta?

    A The First Barons' War
    B The Second Barons' War
    C The Hundred Years' War
    D The Anglo-French War

<u>**John (average)**</u>

Q1 King John was buried in which city?

Q2 King John is regarded as being the last ruler of which empire?

Q3 King John became Lord of what in 1177?

Q4 The Treaty of Le Goulet was signed between King John and which other ruler?

Q5 King John is associated with which legendary outlaw?

Q6 King John is commonly regarded as the favourite of which relative?

Q7 Which claimant to the English throne is believed to have been killed on King John's orders?

Q8 King John wanted John de Gray to be appointed to what position in the Church?

Q9 Which future French king was involved in the First Barons' War?

Q10 What did King John lose just before his death?

<u>**John (expert)**</u>

Q1 The Battle of Bouvines was the concluding battle of which war?

Q2 King John had his marriage to who annulled in 1199?

Q3 When Richard I became King of England, John was granted extensive lands in an attempt to do what?

Q4 How did Arthur I, Duke of Brittany have a claim to the English throne?

Q5 How many legitimate children did King John have?

Q6 In what years did the French invasion of Normandy take place?

Q7 William de Braose was what kind of lord?

Q8 William Marshal, Earl of Pembroke was a knight who served which five English kings?

Q9 King John married his illegitimate daughter Joan to which Welsh prince?

Q10 Which uprising occurred in 1211?

<u>**Henry III (average)**</u>

Q1 Henry III was known by what other name?

Q2 Henry III inherited the English throne in the middle of which war?

Q3 Which kingdom did Henry III invade in 1230?

Q4 Who was Henry III's wife?

Q5 Simon de Montfort was Earl of what?

Q6 Henry III adopted which former English king as his patron saint?

Q7 The Statute of Jewry attempted to segregate which group?

Q8 In what year were the Provisions of Westminster drawn up?

Q9 Which key nobleman was killed at the Battle of Evesham?

Q10 Which short-lived university was founded by Henry III in 1261?

Edward I (average)

Q1 Edward I had the Eleanor crosses erected in memory of who?

Q2 What were Edward I's two nicknames?

Q3 The Edict of Expulsion was a royal decree issued by Edward I expelling what group from England?

Q4 Edward I launched a conquest of what country in the early stages of his reign?

Q5 The Auld Alliance was an alliance between which two kingdoms?

Q6 Which crusade did Edward I take part in?

Q7 What title did Llywelyn ap Gruffudd possess until his death in 1282?

Q8 Edward I is credited with launching an extensive building project of what in Wales?

Q9 Which war broke out in 1296?

Q10 Where was William Wallace executed?

<u>**Edward II (average)**</u>

Q1 How was Edward II allegedly murdered?

Q2 Which nobleman, originating from Gascony, did Edward II have a controversial relationship with?

Q3 Edward II's army was defeated by which Scottish king at the Battle of Bannockburn?

Q4 Edward II's wife famously had an affair with which nobleman?

Q5 Which father and son favourites of Edward II were executed in 1326?

Q6 In what year was the Battle of Boroughbridge fought?

Q7 Where is Edward II buried?

Q8 Who did Edward II abdicate in favour of?

Q9 Which regulations, passed in 1311, aimed to restrict the powers of the king?

Q10 Thomas, Earl of Lancaster was executed near which castle?

Edward III (average)

Q1 Which long-lasting conflict began during Edward III's reign?

Q2 Edward III started to rule independently when he had Roger Mortimer arrested at which castle in 1330?

Q3 How was Alice Perrers associated with Edward III?

Q4 What reached England in 1348?

Q5 For much of his life Edward III was a claimant to which throne?

Q6 What was the name of Edward III's eldest son?

Q7 Who was Edward III's wife?

Q8 Which two major military victories occurred during Edward III's reign?

Q9 The Battle of Sluys was what kind of battle?

Q10 The Treaty of Brétigny was agreed between Edward III and which other king?

<u>**Richard II (easy)**</u>

Q1 What was the personal symbol of Richard II?

  A Lion
  B White Boar
  C White Hart
  D Golden Eagle

Q2 The portrait of Richard II – the oldest surviving portrait of an English monarch –
is on display where?

  A British Museum
  B Buckingham Palace
  C Windsor Castle
  D Westminster Abbey

Q3 How long did Richard II survive after being deposed?

  A Under a year
  B 2 years
  C 10 years
  D 20 years

Q4 Richard II was the grandson of which English king?

  A Edward I
  B Edward II
  C Edward III
  D Richard I

Q5 How old was Richard II when the Peasants' Revolt broke out?

  A 4
  B 14
  C 22
  D 38

Q6 In which castle did Richard II die?

    A Pontefract Castle
    B Middleham Castle
    C Tower of London
    D Nottingham Castle

Q7 What was the name of the schism that occurred in the Catholic Church during Richard II's reign?

    A The Roman Schism
    B Pope Urban's Schism
    C The Western Schism
    D King Richard's Schism

Q8 Which country did Richard II invade in July 1385?

    A Ireland
    B Scotland
    C France
    D Norway

Q9 How was Anne of Bohemia related to Richard II?

    A Wife
    B Sister
    C Mother
    D Aunt

Q10 The period 1397-99 is often referred to by historians as what?

    A The Revolution
    B The Age of Absolutism
    C The Tyranny
    D The Terror

<u>**Richard II (average)**</u>

Q1 How many times did Richard II marry?

Q2 Who was Richard II's father?

Q3 Which rebel leader did Richard II confront at Smithfield?

Q4 Which hall was extensively rebuilt during Richard II's reign?

Q5 *The Canterbury Tales* was written by which author during Richard II's reign?

Q6 What type of tax sparked the Peasants' Revolt?

Q7 What was the name of the Archbishop of Canterbury who was executed during the Peasants' Revolt?

Q8 What long-lasting war with France continued throughout Richard II's reign?

Q9 Thomas of Woodstock, Duke of Gloucester was murdered in which port town?

Q10 Who were the three original Lords Appellant?

<u>**Richard II (expert)**</u>

Q1 Richard II's mother, Joan, was known as the 'Fair Maid' of which English county?

Q2 What was the name of John of Gaunt's London residence, which was burnt down during the Peasants' Revolt?

Q3 What is Thomas Walsingham known for?

Q4 In what year did the Wonderful Parliament take place?

Q5 What was the name of the Lord Mayor of London who killed Wat Tyler?

Q6 In what year did the Merciless Parliament take place?

Q7 Where was Richard II born?

Q8 How old was Richard II when he came to power?

Q9 In what year did Richard II invade Ireland?

Q10 Richard II's second wife, Isabella of Valois, was the daughter of which king?

<u>**Henry IV (average)**</u>

Q1 Henry IV was known by what other name?

Q2 What relation was Richard II to Henry IV?

Q3 Which other English king was born in the same year as Henry IV (1367)?

Q4 Henry IV was the first person from which royal house to be King of England?

Q5 Which powerful nobleman was Henry IV's father?

Q6 How many times did Henry IV marry?

Q7 In what years did the Epiphany Rising occur?

Q8 Henry IV was a member of which group of noblemen during the reign of Richard II?

Q9 Henry IV defeated a rebel army led by who at the Battle of Shrewsbury?

Q10 Where was Henry IV buried?

<u>**Henry V (average)**</u>

Q1 By what other name was Henry V known?

Q2 In what year did the Battle of Agincourt take place?

Q3 What was agreed in the Treaty of Troyes?

Q4 What was John Bradmore's occupation at Henry V's court?

Q5 The estranged friend of Henry V, John Oldcastle, was associated with which religious movement?

Q6 The Treaty of Canterbury was a diplomatic agreement between the Kingdom of England and which empire?

Q7 The Siege of Harfleur occurred in what year?

Q8 What is Henry V believed to have died from?

Q9 How many children did Henry V have?

Q10 The Southampton Plot of 1415 was a conspiracy to replace Henry V with who as King of England?

<u>**Henry VI (easy)**</u>

Q1 As well as being King of England, which other kingdom did Henry VI rule?

A Kingdom of France
B Kingdom of Navarre
C Kingdom of Castile
D Kingdom of Portugal

Q2 How many children did Henry VI have?

A 0
B 1
C 3
D 8

Q3 Which church was Henry VI a member of?

A Anglican
B Catholic
C Methodist
D Orthodox

Q4 How was Joan of Arc executed?

A Stoned
B Hung, drawn and quartered
C Burned at the stake
D Guillotined

Q5 Which civil war broke out during Henry VI's reign?

A The Anarchy
B The Glorious Revolution
C The English Civil War
D The Wars of the Roses

Q6 Which royal house was Henry VI a member of?

A York
B Lancaster
C Blois
D Orange-Nassau

Q7 William Shakespeare's *Henry VI* consists of how many plays?

A 1
B 2
C 3
D 4

Q8 Henry VI suffered from bouts of what?

A Depression
B Paranoia
C Madness
D Rage

Q9 Where was William de la Pole executed?

A Tower of London
B Pontefract Castle
C Tyburn
D English Channel

Q10 The Loveday of 1458 took place at which cathedral?

A St Paul's Cathedral
B Winchester Cathedral
C Salisbury Cathedral
D Leicester Cathedral

Q1 Who was Henry VI's wife?

Q2 Where did Henry VI die?

Q3 On how many occasions did Henry VI serve as King of England?

Q4 Where was Henry VI crowned King of France?

Q5 What was the name of Henry VI's heir?

Q6 Henry VI was liberated from his state of imprisonment in which 1461 battle?

Q7 Henry VI is buried in which castle?

Q8 Who paid the ransom for Margaret of Anjou's release in 1475?

Q9 How old was Henry VI when he became King of England?

Q10 Which long-lasting war ended during Henry VI's reign?

<u>**Henry VI (expert)**</u>

Q1 Which three educational establishments did Henry VI establish?

Q2 What was Joan of Arc's nickname?

Q3 Who was declared Regent of France following the death of Henry V?

Q4 The Congress of Arras was held in what year?

Q5 The favourite of Henry VI, William de la Pole, was Duke of what?

Q6 Jack Cade's Rebellion occurred in what year?

Q7 The Readeption refers to what event?

Q8 Who is Margaret of Anjou buried next to?

Q9 At which 1460 battle was Henry VI captured?

Q10 What relation was Charles VI (the Mad) of France to Henry VI?

<u>Edward IV (average)</u>

Q1 Edward IV's father and which other close relative were killed at the Battle of Wakefield?

Q2 Who was Edward IV's wife?

Q3 How many times did Edward IV serve as King of England?

Q4 Edward IV was the first English king from which royal house?

Q5 Which brother did Edward IV have executed?

Q6 Which Lancastrian heir to the English throne was killed at the Battle of Tewkesbury?

Q7 In what year was Edward IV's heir, the future Edward V, born?

Q8 Which nobleman played a key role in installing Edward IV on the English throne, but later turned against him?

Q9 In what county did the Battle of Mortimer's Cross take place?

Q10 Where was Edward IV born?

Edward V (average)

Q1 What was the name of Edward V's younger brother?

Q2 In what year did Edward V briefly reign?

Q3 What position did the future Richard III hold during Edward V's reign?

Q4 Before becoming king, where was Edward V's court based?

Q5 Edward V was declared illegitimate in which Act of Parliament?

Q6 Where was Edward V and his brother held after his deposition?

Q7 Where was Edward V born?

Q8 Who was in charge of Edward V's upbringing?

Q9 Which physician attended to Edward V?

Q10 Which Tudor historian claimed Edward V and his brother were murdered at midnight on Richard III's orders?

<u>**Richard III (easy)**</u>

Q1 Who was Richard III defeated by at the Battle of Bosworth Field?

A Henry VI
B Henry VII
C Edward IV
D Edward V

Q2 Before becoming king, Richard III was the Duke of what?

A Edinburgh
B York
C Kent
D Gloucester

Q3 Richard III was the final English king from which royal house?

A Lancaster
B York
C Tudor
D Windsor

Q4 Where is Richard III buried?

A York Minster
B Westminster Abbey
C Leicester Cathedral
D Salisbury Cathedral

Q5 What relation were the Princes in the Tower to Richard III?

A Sons
B Cousins
C Brothers
D Nephews

Q6 What was the name of the Tudor historian who wrote *The History of King Richard the Third*?

A Thomas More
B Thomas Cromwell
C Dominic Mancini
D Desiderius Erasmus

Q7 Which county is Richard III most commonly associated with?

A Rutland
B Shropshire
C Herefordshire
D Yorkshire

Q8 What was Richard III's religion?

A Catholic
B Protestant
C Orthodox
D Presbyterian

Q9 In what year did Richard III become King of England?

A 1470
B 1483
C 1485
D 1490

Q10 Richard III is the main protagonist in which William Shakespeare play?

A The Princes in the Tower
B Bosworth
C Richard III
D Tudor

Richard III (average)

Q1 In what year was the Battle of Bosworth fought?

Q2 What was Richard III's personal badge?

Q3 What was the name of Richard III's legitimate son?

Q4 Richard III's wife was a daughter of which nobleman?

Q5 Who led an unsuccessful rebellion against Richard III in the autumn of 1483?

Q6 Who did Richard III depose to become King of England?

Q7 Richard III's demise marked the end of which protracted conflict?

Q8 How many of Richard III's brothers served as King of England?

Q9 Which Archbishop of Canterbury crowned Richard III King of England?

Q10 In what year was Richard III's first and only parliament held?

<u>**Richard III (expert)**</u>

Q1 Which university played an instrumental role in the discovery of Richard III's body?

Q2 In what town did Richard III have Anthony Woodville, Earl Rivers (amongst other members of Edward V's household) arrested?

Q3 Which 1484 Act of Parliament legitimised Richard III's claim to the throne?

Q4 Which powerful nobleman was hastily executed after a meeting of the royal council at the Tower of London on 13 June 1483?

Q5 Which bishop provided evidence that led to Edward IV and Elizabeth Woodville's marriage to be declared bigamous?

Q6 Which nobleman's intervention at the Battle of Bosworth ultimately led to Richard III's defeat?

Q7 William Collingbourne's famous lampoon 'The Catte, the Ratte and Lovell our dogge rulyth all Englande under a hogge' attacked Richard III and three of his supporters. Who were they?

Q8 During his adolescence, Richard III developed what condition?

Q9 When Edward IV died, what did Richard III become?

Q10 Who was Richard III's main rival in the north of England?

Q1 Who was Henry VII's mother?

Q2 Which king did Henry VII defeat at Bosworth Field?

Q3 Which castle was Henry VII born at?

Q4 Henry VII founded which royal dynasty?

Q5 From which country did Henry VII descend?

Q6 Who pretended to be Edward Plantagenet, Earl of Warwick in 1487?

Q7 Perkin Warbeck was born in which present-day country?

Q8 Who was Henry VII's oldest legitimate son?

Q9 Who did Henry VII marry to unite the Houses of Lancaster and York, ultimately bringing an end to the Wars of the Roses?

Q10 What relation was Jasper Tudor to Henry VII?

<u>Henry VIII (easy)</u>

Q1 How many wives did Henry VIII have?

    A 1
    B 2
    C 4
    D 6

Q2 Henry VIII changed England's state religion to what?

    A Catholicism
    B Orthodoxy
    C Protestantism
    D Judaism

Q3 In the early stages of his reign, Henry VIII was referred to as the 'Defender of the' what?

    A Faith
    B Kingdom
    C Crown
    D People

Q4 How many of Henry VIII's children went on to rule England?

    A 0
    B 1
    C 2
    D 3

Q5 The 'Dissolution of the' what occurred from 1536 onwards?

    A Parliament
    B Monasteries
    C Clergy
    D Council

Q6 Which kingdom did Henry VIII fight against at the Battle of the Spurs?

   A Kingdom of Spain
   B Kingdom of the Netherlands
   C Kingdom of Bulgaria
   D Kingdom of France

Q7 Henry's will designated how many executors to serve on a council of regency until Edward VI reached the age of 18?

   A 1
   B 5
   C 10
   D 16

Q8 Which monarch, over 100 years after Henry VIII's death, was buried in the same vault?

   A Elizabeth I of England
   B James I of England
   C Charles I of England
   D Charles II of England

Q9 The Rough Wooing was a war between the Kingdom of England and which other kingdom?

   A Kingdom of Ireland
   B Kingdom of Spain
   C Kingdom of Scotland
   D Kingdom of France

Q10 What was the *Mary Rose*?

   A Crown
   B Chapel
   C Relic
   D Ship

<u>**Henry VIII (average)**</u>

Q1 Which of Henry VIII's wives is buried alongside him in St. George's chapel in Windsor Castle?

Q2 Which of Henry VIII's wives were executed?

Q3 Which position did Henry VIII create and appoint himself to in the Church of England?

Q4 Which author and statesman was executed in 1535?

Q5 The Crown of Ireland Act 1542 created what title?

Q6 Who were Catherine of Aragon's parents?

Q7 Which pope refused to annul Henry VIII's marriage to Catherine of Aragon?

Q8 In which palace did Henry VIII die?

Q9 What method of execution was used for the wives Henry VIII condemned to death?

Q10 In what year did Henry VIII become King of England?

<u>**Henry VIII (expert)**</u>

Q1 Under which acts were England and Wales legally unified?

Q2 In what year was the Royal Navy founded?

Q3 Which wife was Henry VIII married to the longest?

Q4 What was the name of Henry VIII's first son?

Q5 The Treaty of London (1518) was what kind of pact?

Q6 What theological treatise did Henry VIII publish in 1521?

Q7 Mark Smeaton was executed for committing adultery with who?

Q8 Thomas Cromwell served as Governor of which island?

Q9 The Treasons Act 1534 made it treason to do what?

Q10 Who baptised Henry VIII?

<u>Edward VI (average)</u>

Q1 Who was Edward VI's mother?

Q2 Edward VI was a devout follower of which form of Christianity?

Q3 Which noble was educated at Henry VIII's court and became a close friend of Edward VI?

Q4 Edward VI appears in which Mark Twain novel?

Q5 How was Lady Jane Grey related to Edward VI?

Q6 Who dominated politics in the early stages of Edward VI's reign?

Q7 How old was Edward VI when he died?

Q8 Who did the Kingdom of England fight at the Battle of Pinkie Cleugh?

Q9 Where was Edward VI born?

Q10 Henry VIII's will named how many executors, who were to act as Edward's Council until he reached the age of eighteen?

<u>**Mary I (average)**</u>

Q1 Mary I was an ardent supporter of what church?

Q2 Who was Mary I's husband?

Q3 Who was Mary I's mother?

Q4 What nickname is commonly given to Mary I?

Q5 Who was briefly proclaimed Queen of England after the death of Edward VI?

Q6 How many children did Mary I have?

Q7 Which powerful nobleman was executed on 22 August 1553?

Q8 What was the name of the popular uprising that occurred in 1554?

Q9 Which Archbishop of Canterbury was executed during Mary I's reign?

Q10 The Siege of Calais occurred in what year?

<u>**Elizabeth I (easy)**</u>

Q1 Elizabeth I was the last English monarch from which royal house?

    A Plantagenet
    B Tudor
    C Stuart
    D Orange-Nassau

Q2 Who was Elizabeth I's mother?

    A Catherine of Aragon
    B Anne of Cleves
    C Catherine Parr
    D Anne Boleyn

Q3 England was converted back to what during Elizabeth I's reign?

    A Catholicism
    B Orthodoxy
    C Lollardism
    D Protestantism

Q4 Which conflict occurred between 1585 and 1604?

    A Anglo-Spanish War
    B Anglo-Dutch War
    C Thirty Years' War
    D War of the Austrian Succession

Q5 How many ships were there in the Spanish Armada?

    A 15
    B 50
    C 130
    D 300

Q6 How many times did Elizabeth I marry?

A 0
B 1
C 2
D 3

Q7 What was Francis Drake's occupation?

A Executioner
B Academic
C Advisor
D Privateer

Q8 The ruler of which kingdom succeeded Elizabeth I?

A Kingdom of France
B Kingdom of Bohemia
C Kingdom of Scotland
D Kingdom of Denmark

Q9 Simon Renard was an ambassador serving which kingdom?

A Kingdom of Spain
B Kingdom of England
C Kingdom of France
D Kingdom of Portugal

Q10 Elizabeth I's favourite, Robert Dudley, was Earl of what?

A Rutland
B Wessex
C Leicester
D Northumberland

<u>Elizabeth I (average)</u>

Q1 In her later years, what did Elizabeth I refuse to have in any of her rooms?

Q2 Name one of Elizabeth I's nicknames.

Q3 Who was Elizabeth I's chief advisor for the majority of her reign?

Q4 Elizabeth I was responsible for the execution of which Scottish monarch?

Q5 In what year was the Spanish Armada defeated?

Q6 Which world-renowned playwright rose to prominence during Elizabeth I's reign?

Q7 Francis Drake famously captained which galleon?

Q8 Ingram Frizer is well-known for reportedly killing who?

Q9 Elizabeth I courted which Duke of Anjou?

Q10 In which palace did Elizabeth I die?

<u>**Elizabeth I (expert)**</u>

Q1 The Act of Supremacy 1558 replaced what act that had been passed by Henry VIII and repealed by Mary I?

Q2 Who commanded the Spanish Armada?

Q3 What was Christopher Marlowe's occupation?

Q4 Who was Elizabeth I's first governess?

Q5 Katherine Champernowne was known by what name to Elizabeth I?

Q6 Which 1543 act was revoked in Edward VI's will?

Q7 How old was Elizabeth I when she became Queen of England?

Q8 Who crowned Elizabeth I Queen of England?

Q9 How were Elizabeth I and Mary, Queen of Scots related?

Q10 Which Moroccan ambassador visited England in 1600?

Q1 Who was the leader of the Gunpowder Plot?

    A Guy Fawkes
    B Robert Catesby
    C Thomas Percy
    D Robert Keyes

Q2 Before becoming King of England, what other kingdom was James I king of?

    A France
    B The Netherlands
    C Scotland
    D Sweden

Q3 James I was the first English king from which royal house?

    A Plantagenet
    B Tudor
    C Stuart
    D Hanover

Q4 In what year was the *King James Bible* published

    A 1605
    B 1611
    C 1615
    D 1620

Q5 In what year did James I become King of England?

    A 1583
    B 1590
    C 1603
    D 1605

Q6 How old was James I when he first became a king?

  A 1
  B 5
  C 18
  D 23

Q7 What was the name of James I's wife?

  A Marie Antoinette
  B Eleanor of Aquitaine
  C Margaret of Anjou
  D Anne of Denmark

Q8 What caused the death of James I's father, Henry Stuart, Lord Darnley?

  A Smallpox
  B Murder
  C Heart attack
  D Starvation

Q9 Where was James I born?

  A Tower of London
  B Stirling Castle
  C Conwy Castle
  D Edinburgh Castle

Q10 Robert Cecil served as Secretary of what between 1596 and 1612?

  A Defence
  B State
  C Treasury
  D Colonial Affairs

<u>James I (average)</u>

Q1 Who was James I's mother?

Q2 What name is given to the era when James I was King of England?

Q3 What did James I want to do to the English and Scottish Parliaments?

Q4 The English colonisation of where commenced during James I's reign?

Q5 On what date in 1605 did the Gunpowder Plot occur?

Q6 Who was James I's eldest son?

Q7 What was the name of the Duke of Buckingham, the favourite and alleged lover of James I?

Q8 Sir Walter Raleigh was executed in what year of James I's reign?

Q9 How was Guy Fawkes executed?

Q10 Which major European war took place during James I's reign?

<u>**James I (expert)**</u>

Q1 James I was the great-great-grandson of which king?

Q2 What was the name of the philosophical dissertation that James I published in 1597?

Q3 James Hamilton assassinated which Regent of Scotland before James I came into his majority?

Q4 The Main Plot was an alleged conspiracy to replace James I with who?

Q5 The Gentleman Adventurers of Fife were awarded lands on what island by James I?

Q6 The Addled Parliament took place in what year?

Q7 What was the occupation of Inigo Jones?

Q8 In what year was the Globe Theatre destroyed by a fire?

Q9 The Millenary Petition was a list of requests given to James I by who?

Q10 What began in Ulster during the reign of James I?

<u>**Charles I (easy)**</u>

Q1 Which conflict took place during Charles I's reign?

    A The Anarchy
    B The English Civil War
    C The Wars of the Roses
    D The American Revolution

Q2 In what country was Charles I born?

    A England
    B Ireland
    C Scotland
    D France

Q3 How many of Charles I's children went on to become King of England?

    A 0
    B 1
    C 2
    D 3

Q4 In what year was Charles I executed?

    A 1630
    B 1649
    C 1660
    D 1672

Q5 Who governed England after Charles I's execution?

    A Charles II
    B Queen Henrietta Maria
    C Thomas Fairfax
    D Oliver Cromwell

Q6 Who was the Parliamentary commander-in-chief?

    A Oliver Cromwell
    B John Pym
    C John Hampden
    D Thomas Fairfax

Q7 In which castle was Charles I imprisoned?

    A Carisbrooke Castle
    B Nottingham Castle
    C Pontefract Castle
    D Balmoral Castle

Q8 The Wars of the Three Kingdoms took place in which kingdoms?

    A England, Scotland and France
    B England, Scotland and Spain
    C England, Scotland and Ireland
    D England, Ireland and France

Q9 The Grand Remonstrance was a list of grievances presented to Charles I by who?

    A His wife
    B His sons
    C The Pope
    D The English Parliament

Q10 How was Charles I executed?

    A Beheaded
    B Hung
    C Boiled
    D Burned

Charles I (average)

Q1 What was the name of Charles I's wife?

Q2 The Roundheads were supporters of who during the English Civil War?

Q3 What was the Kingdom of England referred to as between 1649 and 1660?

Q4 Charles I was executed outside which palace?

Q5 What was the name of the army that was created by the Parliamentarians during the English Civil War?

Q6 The period from 1629 to 1640 is known by what name?

Q7 On what charge was Charles I executed for?

Q8 The Battle of Marston Moor was fought in which county?

Q9 Apart from Charles I, who was the most prominent royalist leader in the English Civil War?

Q10 Who was Charles I's youngest son?

<u>**Charles I (expert)**</u>

Q1 Charles I raised his army in the English Civil War by using what medieval method?

Q2 Charles I was a staunch supporter of what political and religious doctrine of royal and political legitimacy?

Q3 Which Archbishop of Canterbury was executed in 1645?

Q4 In which pub was George Villiers, Duke of Buckingham assassinated?

Q5 Who were the 'Five Members' from the House of Commons who Charles I attempted to have arrested in 1642?

Q6 How many English Civil Wars were there between 1642 and 1651?

Q7 The Bishops' Wars of 1639 and 1640 were fought between Scottish Royalists and who else?

Q8 *Charles I in Three Positions* is a painting of Charles I by which Flemish artist?

Q9 John Hampden was mortally wounded at which battle?

Q10 Pride's Purge preceded which parliament?

<u>**Charles II (average)**</u>

Q1 The Popish Plot was a fictitious conspiracy concocted by who?

Q2 What is the period called between Charles I's execution and Charles II's rise to power?

Q3 In what year did the Restoration begin?

Q4 Charles II was defeated by who at the Battle of Worcester?

Q5 How was Moll Davis associated with Charles II?

Q6 The Cavalier Parliament endured just under how many years?

Q7 The Rye House Plot of 1683 was a plot to do what?

Q8 Charles II was known as the Merry what?

Q9 How many children did Charles II have with his wife Catherine of Braganza?

Q10 Charles II accompanied his father to which 1642 battle?

James II (average)

Q1 James II was deposed in which revolution?

Q2 James II was the last king of which faith to rule England?

Q3 The birth of which prince precipitated James II's downfall?

Q4 Before James II, how many other Stuart monarchs had been deposed in England?

Q5 Which political movement aimed to restore James II and his heirs to the English throne?

Q6 In which country did James II die?

Q7 Which king did James II fight at the Battle of the Boyne?

Q8 Which king offered James II asylum?

Q9 The Seven Bishops were imprisoned for their opposition to which proclamations made by James II?

Q10 How was James II related to his predecessor, Charles II?

<u>**William III and Mary II (average)**</u>

Q1 William III was better known by what name?

Q2 In which republic was William III born?

Q3 Who was Mary II's father?

Q4 What religion did both William III and Mary II adhere to?

Q5 Did William III or Mary II reign longer?

Q6 In which palace did both William III and Mary II die?

Q7 The Bill of Rights was passed in what year?

Q8 The seven English noblemen who wrote to William III, inviting him to invade England, were later named what?

Q9 Henry Compton, who crowned William III and Mary II King and Queen of England, held what position in the church?

Q10 *Music for the Funeral of Queen Mary* was composed by who?

<u>**Anne (easy)**</u>

Q1 Anne was the first Queen of what?

    A England
    B Great Britain
    C Ireland
    D Isle of Mann

Q2 Where is Anne buried?

    A St Paul's Cathedral
    B Windsor Castle
    C York Minster
    D Westminster Abbey

Q3 What church was Anne a member of?

    A Catholic
    B Orthodox
    C Presbyterian
    D Church of England

Q4 What royal house was Anne a member of?

    A Plantagenet
    B Tudor
    C Stuart
    D Windsor

Q5 Who was Anne's only child to survive infancy?

    A Prince William, Duke of Gloucester
    B Prince Richard, Duke of York
    C Edward, Prince of Wales
    D James, Earl of Shrewsbury

Q6 In what year was Anne's coronation?

    A 1700
    B 1702
    C 1707
    D 1710

Q7 Which party gained a majority in the House of Commons in the 1708 general election?

    A Whig
    B Liberal
    C Tory
    D Labour

Q8 Which war took place during Anne's reign?

    A Crimean War
    B War of the Spanish Succession
    C Napoleonic Wars
    D Seven Years' War

Q9 Who instigated an uprising in 1715?

    A Jacobites
    B Puritans
    C Luddites
    D Socialists

Q10 In what year did Anne first fall pregnant?

    A 1675
    B 1680
    C 1684
    D 1700

<u>**Anne (average)**</u>

Q1 Which palace was Anne born in?

Q2 Which political party did Anne favour?

Q3 In what years were the two Acts of Union passed?

Q4 How was Anne related to Mary II?

Q5 Anne's husband, Prince George, was from which country?

Q6 Immediately following her marriage, where did Anne and her husband reside?

Q7 Shortly after her accession, what position did Anne appoint her husband to?

Q8 The 'Great Storm' struck southern England in which year of Anne's reign?

Q9 Which traditional religious practice did Anne reinstitute?

Q10 How were Anne and her successor, George I, related?

<u>**Anne (expert)**</u>

Q1 Sarah Churchill, an estranged friend of Anne, held which title?

Q2 Anne's mother, Anne Hyde, was the first wife of who?

Q3 As a child, Anne suffered from a medical condition affecting which part of the body?

Q4 Prince William, Duke of Gloucester was how old when he died?

Q5 How many times did Anne fall pregnant?

Q6 At the start of Anne's reign, what position in government did Robert Harley hold?

Q7 What name was given to the group of Whig politicians who were seen to direct the management of the Whig Party during the reigns of William III and Anne?

Q8 John Somers held which political office between 1708 and 1710?

Q9 Who was Archbishop of Canterbury during Anne's reign?

Q10 In what year did Anne become Princess Anne of Denmark?

<u>**George I (easy)**</u>

Q1 What was George I's primary title before becoming King of Great Britain?

    A Pope
    B Elector of Hanover
    C Holy Roman Emperor
    D Earl of Northumberland

Q2 Who became Britain's first de facto prime minister during George I's reign?

    A Winston Churchill
    B William Pitt the Elder
    C William Gladstone
    D Robert Walpole

Q3 How many wives did George I have?

    A 0
    B 1
    C 2
    D 3

Q4 The Jacobite, John Erskine, was from which country?

    A England
    B Ireland
    C Wales
    D Scotland

Q5 For what main reason was George I disliked by the British?

    A He was Catholic
    B He was authoritarian
    C He was German
    D He was greedy

Q6 George I was a great grandson of which English monarch?

A James I
B James II
C Charles I
D Charles II

Q7 How many members of the House of Hanover ruled Great Britain?

A 1
B 4
C 6
D 9

Q8 The War of the Quadruple Alliance pitted a coalition of countries (Britain, France, the Holy Roman Empire and the Dutch Republic) against which kingdom?

A Portugal
B Spain
C Bulgaria
D Russia

Q9 As well as being his wife, what relation was Sophia Dorothea of Celle to George I?

A Sister
B Cousin
C Second Cousin
D Stepmother

Q10 During George I's reign, who was the main Catholic claimant to the throne of Great Britain?

A James II of England
B Henry Benedict Stuart
C Mary of Modena
D James Francis Edward Stuart

<u>**George I (average)**</u>

Q1 What political party did the first British Prime Minister belong to?

Q2 What royal house did George I belong to?

Q3 George I served at the Battle of Vienna during which war?

Q4 Melusine von der Schulenburg was associated with George I in what way?

Q5 What occurred alongside George I's coronation in over 20 English towns?

Q6 In which stately home did George I have his wife, Sophia Dorothea of Celle, imprisoned?

Q7 What was the main difference between governing Britain and governing Hanover?

Q8 Which 1701 Act of Parliament ultimately led to George I becoming King of Great Britain?

Q9 What did George I die from?

Q10 What branch of Christianity did George I adhere to?

George I (expert)

Q1 In which city did George I die?

Q2 How old was George I when he ascended the British throne?

Q3 Who did George I's wife, Sophia Dorothea of Celle, allegedly have an affair with?

Q4 In 1717 George I contributed to the establishment of which anti-Spanish league?

Q5 In which chapel was George I initially buried?

Q6 Which nobleman led the 1715 Jacobite uprising?

Q7 The Septennial Act 1716 increased the maximum length of a parliament from 3 years to how many?

Q8 Who did George I refuse to have as regent of Great Britain when, on a number of occasions, he returned to Hanover?

Q9 What was George I's father's name?

Q10 What was George I's middle name?

<u>**George II (easy)**</u>

Q1 How was George II's successor, George III, related to him?

A Son
B Grandson
C Nephew
D Brother

Q2 Both of George II's parents committed what sin?

A Murder
B Charlatanism
C Adultery
D Blasphemy

Q3 How old was George II when he became King of Great Britain?

A 9
B 23
C 43
D 62

Q4 *Music for the Royal Fireworks* was composed to celebrate the end of which war?

A The War of Austrian Succession
B The War of Spanish Succession
C Seven Years' War
D Crimean War

Q5 George II is the most recent British monarch to be buried where?

A Windsor Castle
B Westminster Abbey
C St Paul's Cathedral
D Sandringham Estate

Q6 George II donated the royal library to which museum in 1757?

    A British Museum
    B Natural History Museum
    C The National Gallery
    D German Historical Museum

Q7 In which major film franchise does George II make an appearance?

    A *Lord of the Rings*
    B *Harry Potter*
    C *The Mummy*
    D *Pirates of the Caribbean*

Q8 How many times did George II marry?

    A 0
    B 1
    C 2
    D 3

Q9 What was George II's full name?

    A George Frederick
    B George James
    C George Augustus
    D George Wilhelm

Q10 George II held what position in the Holy Roman Empire?

    A Prince-elector
    B King
    C Prime minister
    D Bishop

<u>**George II (average)**</u>

Q1 George II was the last British monarch to be born where?

Q2 The last Jacobite rebellion took place in which year of George II's reign?

Q3 Until the age of four, what was the only language George II knew how to speak?

Q4 George II famously had a poor relationship with which relative?

Q5 What was the name of George II's eldest son?

Q6 After his defeat at the Battle of Culloden, Charles Edward Stuart disguised himself as a maid called what?

Q7 In which year did the Seven Years' War break out?

Q8 What was significant about George II dying at the age of 76?

Q9 George II founded the first university in the Electorate of Hanover. What was its name?

Q10 Before he died, George II left instructions for what to be done to his and his wife's coffins?

<u>**George II (expert)**</u>

Q1 George II became the last British monarch to lead his troops in which battle?

Q2 In which palace did George II die?

Q3 In which 1705 Act of Parliament was George II naturalised as an English subject?

Q4 Which composer composed *Zadok the Priest* for George II's coronation?

Q5 The Annus Mirabilis of 1759 refers to what?

Q6 In what year of George II's reign did the French plan to invade Britain?

Q7 A post-mortem revealed George II had died as a result of what?

Q8 George II served as the chancellor of which college?

Q9 A statue of George II by the Flemish sculptor John Van Nost stands in which London square?

Q10 Which asteroid was named after George II?

<u>**George III (easy)**</u>

Q1 In what year did the acts come into force that united the Kingdom of Great Britain and the Kingdom of Ireland?

    A 1790
    B 1795
    C 1801
    D 1809

Q2 George III assumed which title in Hanover in 1814?

    A Prince of Hanover
    B Elector of Hanover
    C Emperor of Hanover
    D King of Hanover

Q3 Unlike his two predecessors what was George III's first language?

    A English
    B German
    C French
    D Latin

Q4 Key colonies on which continent were lost during George III's reign?

    A Asia
    B Africa
    C North America
    D South America

Q5 How many children did George III and his wife have?

    A 0
    B 1
    C 3
    D 15

Q6 William Pitt the Elder acquired which title from George III?

    A Duke of York
    B Earl of Chatham
    C Earl of Wessex
    D Prince of Wales

Q7 The Intolerable Acts were passed following which event?

    A Declaration of Independence
    B Battle of Trafalgar
    C Siege of Yorktown
    D Boston Tea Party

Q8 The Gordon Riots of 1780 were based on what sentiments?

    A Pro-democracy
    B Pro-royalty
    C Anti-Catholic
    D Anti-Puritan

Q9 How many Pitts served as Prime Minister during George III's reign?

    A 0
    B 1
    C 2
    D 3

Q10 Who attempted to assassinate George III in 1800?

    A John Wilkes Booth
    B Lee Harvey Oswald
    C James Hadfield
    D James Earl Ray

<u>**George III (average)**</u>

Q1 How many times did George III visit Hanover?

Q2 Which European ruler threatened to invade Britain during George III's reign?

Q3 In the latter part of his life, George III suffered from what kind of illness?

Q4 Who ruled as George III's proxy during the Regency era?

Q5 After whose death was the future George III created Prince of Wales?

Q6 The King's Library, assembled by George III, was one of the most important collections of books and pamphlets of which intellectual and philosophical movement?

Q7 Who successfully persuaded George III not to marry Lady Sarah Lennox?

Q8 The Royal Proclamation of 1763 restricted the westward expansion of what?

Q9 'No taxation without representation' was a key grievance of citizens of which group of colonies?

Q10 Who was the first United States Ambassador to the United Kingdom?

<u>**George III (expert)**</u>

Q1 In which house was George III born?

Q2 At the age of 10, George III took part in a family production of which Joseph Addison play?

Q3 In which duchy was George III's wife born?

Q4 Who served as the first Scottish Prime Minister of Great Britain between 1762 and 1763?

Q5 The radical newspaper *The North Briton* is associated with which Member of Parliament?

Q6 Which Prime Minister led Britain through the majority of the American Revolutionary War?

Q7 The Royal Marriages Act 1772 was repealed as a result of which 2011 agreement?

Q8 George III allegedly shook hands with a tree, mistakenly believing it to be who?

Q9 Which Lincolnshire physician is known for treating George III?

Q10 The Ministry of All the Talents was a government of national unity formed by which Prime Minister?

<u>**George IV (average)**</u>

Q1 What did George IV commission John Nash to build in Brighton?

Q2 How many years did George IV's reign last?

Q3 What was the name of George IV's wife?

Q4 How was George IV related to his successor, William IV?

Q5 The Pains and Penalties Bill was introduced to Parliament in 1820 at the request of George IV in an attempt to do what?

Q6 How many legitimate children did George IV have?

Q7 Which chapel at Windsor Castle is George IV buried in?

Q8 George IV was baptised by which Archbishop of Canterbury?

Q9 In 1821 George IV became the first monarch to pay a state visit to which country since Richard II?

Q10 Which party governed Britain during George IV's reign?

Q1 Which palace was William IV born in?

Q2 Owing to his service in the Royal Navy, what was William IV nicknamed?

Q3 How many illegitimate children did William IV have with the actress Dorothea Jordan?

Q4 What important act concerning slavery was passed during William IV's reign?

Q5 What relation was the future Queen Victoria to William IV?

Q6 What rank did William IV enter the Royal Navy at when he was thirteen years old?

Q7 Why did William IV attempt to marry Catherine Tylney-Long?

Q8 William IV supported which country's independence?

Q9 Who acted as viceroy of Hanover during William IV's reign?

Q10 The Reform Act 1832 introduced wide-ranging changes to what?

<u>**Victoria (easy)**</u>

Q1 Queen Victoria was the last British monarch from which royal house?

    A Plantagenet
    B Tudor
    C Stuart
    D Hanover

Q2 Queen Victoria wore black for the remainder of her life after the death of which relative?

    A Sister
    B Mother
    C Son
    D Husband

Q3 How many people served as Prime Minister during Queen Victoria's reign?

    A 2
    B 4
    C 10
    D 17

Q4 Queen Victoria was named the 'grandmother' of what?

    A England
    B Queens
    C Europe
    D George

Q5 How many attempts were there to assassinate Queen Victoria?

    A 0
    B 1
    C 3
    D 8

Q6 What did Ireland suffer from between 1845 and 1849?

    A Great Famine
    B Black Death
    C Revolution
    D Mass unemployment

Q7 Which controversial law(s) were repealed in 1846?

    A Poor Laws
    B Corn Laws
    C Treaty of Union
    D Titulus Regius

Q8 How many political parties governed Britain during Queen Victoria's reign?

    A 1
    B 2
    C 3
    D 4

Q9 John Brown, a personal attendant and favourite of Queen Victoria, was from what country?

    A England
    B Germany
    C Ireland
    D Scotland

Q10 The Victoria Cross was introduced in 1856 to reward acts of valour during which war?

    A Crimean War
    B Anglo-Zulu War
    C First Boer War
    D First World War

<u>**Victoria (average)**</u>

Q1 What additional title did Queen Victoria adopt in 1876?

Q2 Which island did Queen Victoria die on?

Q3 What was the name of Queen Victoria's husband?

Q4 At birth, what place was Queen Victoria in the line of succession?

Q5 Who was Prime Minister at the time of Queen Victoria's coronation?

Q6 Whose death in 1839 gave Queen Victoria a negative image?

Q7 Who was Queen Victoria's childhood governess?

Q8 Queen Victoria's youngest son, Leopold, was affected by what disease?

Q9 Which Prime Minister did Queen Victoria have a better relationship with: Benjamin Disraeli or William Gladstone?

Q10 Which joint-stock company was dissolved after the Indian Rebellion of 1857?

<u>**Victoria (expert)**</u>

Q1 How old was Queen Victoria when she inherited the throne?

Q2 How many children did Queen Victoria have?

Q3 Under what set of rules was Queen Victoria raised?

Q4 What was the name of the King Charles Spaniel owned by Queen Victoria during her youth?

Q5 Who became King of Hanover after the death of William IV?

Q6 Approximately how many visitors came to London for Queen Victoria's coronation celebrations?

Q7 Who attempted to assassinate Queen Victoria in 1840?

Q8 In what year was the Anti-Corn Law League founded?

Q9 Whose attempt to assassinate Napoleon III ultimately resulted in Lord Palmerston resigning as Prime Minister?

Q10 Why did Roderick Maclean shoot at Queen Victoria as her carriage left Windsor railway station in 1882?

<u>**Edward VII (average)**</u>

Q1 Edward VII played a role in the modernisation of which Royal Navy fleet?

Q2 Which war was Britain engaged in when Edward VII came to power?

Q3 What name has been given to the era when Edward VII was king?

Q4 Edward VII famously had a poor relationship with which nephew?

Q5 The constitutional crisis Edward VII died in the midst of was resolved by which Act of Parliament?

Q6 The 1909/1910 People's Budget was proposed by which political party?

Q7 Which country was Edward VII's wife born in?

Q8 Where was Edward VII born, and where did he die?

Q9 Edward VII was the first British king from which royal house?

Q10 What caused Edward VII's coronation to be delayed?

<u>**George V (average)**</u>

Q1 Which governess cared for George V's sickly son, Prince John?

Q2 At the start of George V's reign the Parliament Act 1911 established the supremacy of which House of Parliament?

Q3 Which cadet training ship did George V join when he was 12 years old?

Q4 In 1917 what name did George V change his royal house to?

Q5 What was George V's wife called?

Q6 The Commonwealth was originally created through which 1926 declaration?

Q7 In what year did Ramsay MacDonald become the first Labour Prime Minister?

Q8 George V ultimately opposed a government plan to offer which European ruler and his family asylum in 1917?

Q9 In what year did George V make the first royal Christmas speech on the radio?

Q10 George V ordered a portrait of himself by which artist to be burned?

<u>**Edward VIII (average)**</u>

Q1 In what year did Edward VIII serve as King of the United Kingdom?

Q2 On which birthday was the future Edward VIII named Prince of Wales?

Q3 What was the name of the woman Edward VIII abdicated in order to marry?

Q4 In which country did Edward VIII die?

Q5 What title did Edward VIII obtain after his abdication?

Q6 Who did Edward VIII meet, against the advice of the British government, in 1937?

Q7 Field Marshal Horatio Herbert Kitchener refused to allow the future Edward VIII to do what in the First World War?

Q8 Operation Willi refers to an unsuccessful attempt by the German SS to do what?

Q9 In which town is Edward VIII buried?

Q10 Edward VIII had a love affair with which Parisian during the First World War?

George VI (average)

Q1 George VI led the United Kingdom through which war?

Q2 George VI was the first head of what and the last emperor of what?

Q3 What name was George VI known by before his accession?

Q4 After George VI's death, what did people start calling his wife, Elizabeth Angela Marguerite Bowes-Lyon, to avoid confusion?

Q5 In the mid-1920s George VI had what kind of therapy?

Q6 Who was George VI's partner in the 1926 Wimbledon Men's Doubles tournament?

Q7 Which brother of George VI was killed in active service in 1942?

Q8 Who was George VI's preferred choice to replace Neville Chamberlain as Prime Minister?

Q9 George VI addressed which intergovernmental organisation in its first assembly in 1946?

Q10 Who played George VI in the 2010 film *The King's Speech*?

<u>**Elizabeth II (average)**</u>

Q1 Which service did Elizabeth II serve in during the Second World War?

Q2 How many Commonwealth realms is Elizabeth II queen of?

Q3 In 2017 Elizabeth II became the first British monarch to reach which jubilee?

Q4 Which former daughter-in-law of Elizabeth II was killed in a car crash in Paris in 1997?

Q5 Who was Prime Minister when Elizabeth II came to power?

Q6 Who is Elizabeth II's husband?

Q7 Who was Elizabeth II's only sibling?

Q8 Who was Archbishop of Canterbury when Elizabeth II came to power?

Q9 Elizabeth II holds what position in the Church of England?

Q10 In 1983 Elizabeth II was angered when US President Ronald Reagan ordered the invasion of which country?

National and Regional Histories

<u>**Africa 1 (easy)**</u>

Q1 The Scramble for Africa culminated in the outbreak of which war?

    A Second Boer War
    B Crimean War
    C First World War
    D Second World War

Q2 Sundiata Keita founded which empire?

    A Ghana Empire
    B Benin Empire
    C Mali Empire
    D Jolof Empire

Q3 What nationality are Boers associated with?

    A English
    B Dutch
    C French
    D Italian

Q4 Shaka was one of the most influential monarchs of which kingdom?

    A Zulu Kingdom
    B Kingdom of Nri
    C Kingdom of Zimbabwe
    D Kingdom of Kongo

Q5 Which country did Italy invade in 1935?

    A Eritrea
    B Ethiopia
    C Sudan
    D Egypt

Q6 What year is referred to as the Year of Africa?

A 1882
B 1914
C 1947
D 1960

Q7 In what century did the first Muslim conquests occur in northern Africa?

A 2nd century BC
B 1st century AD
C 7th century AD
D 11th century AD

Q8 Hippo Regius is located in which present-day country?

A Tunisia
B Algeria
C Sudan
D Kenya

Q9 Who served as the first King of Madagascar?

A Andrianampoinimerina
B Radama I
C Ranavalona I
D Andrianjafy

Q10 The Kingdom of Imerina dominated which island?

A Mauritius
B Unguja
C Djerba
D Madagascar

<u>**Africa 2 (average)**</u>

Q1 Which UNESCO listed heritage site was the home of Oba of Benin?

Q2 Who led the Emin Pasha Relief Expedition?

Q3 Cape Coast Castle was built in which British colony?

Q4 The Golden Stool was the royal throne of which ethnic group?

Q5 Béhanzin, King of Dahomey lost his throne after an invasion by which country?

Q6 In which country did Cetshwayo kaMpande spend some time in exile?

Q7 A *nome* was a territorial division in which civilisation?

Q8 The Mercenary War was a revolt against which Phoenician state?

Q9 What was the name of the President of Rwanda in 1994, who died after his plane was shot down?

Q10 Great Zimbabwe was the capital of which kingdom?

<u>**Africa 3 (expert)**</u>

Q1 What was the capital city of the Ashanti Empire?

Q2 Who was President of the South African Republic between 1883 and 1902?

Q3 Apartheid was introduced in South Africa following parliamentary elections held in what year?

Q4 Who served as the first President of Tanzania?

Q5 The Second Battle of Dongola was fought between the Rashidun Caliphate and which Nubian kingdom?

Q6 The face of the Great Sphinx of Giza is believed to represent which pharaoh?

Q7 The Manikongo was the title of the ruler of which kingdom?

Q8 Fasil Ghebbi is situated in which Ethiopian city?

Q9 António I of Kongo was decapitated after fighting which battle against the Portuguese?

Q10 In which present-day country did the missionary David Livingstone die?

Q1 For approximately how many years has Australia been inhabited?

    A 100,000 years
    B 60,000 years
    C 10,000 years
    D 700 years

Q2 Who was the first Prime Minister of Australia?

    A Malcom Turnbull
    B Malcolm Fraser
    C Edmund Barton
    D John Curtin

Q3 How many colonies united to form the Commonwealth of Australia?

    A 2
    B 3
    C 6
    D 13

Q4 William Bligh was deposed as Governor of New South Wales during which rebellion?

    A Rum Rebellion
    B Eureka Rebellion
    C Boston Tea Party
    D Stono Rebellion

Q5 Don Bradman is well-known for playing what sport?

    A Football
    B Aussie Rules
    C Rugby
    D Cricket

Q6 The First World War stretcher-bearer John Simpson Kirkpatrick used what kind of animal to carry wounded soldiers to safety?

    A Horse
    B Donkey
    C Camel
    D Giraffe

Q7 Eddie Mabo campaigned for the rights of which group?

    A Women
    B Christians
    C Prisoners
    D Aboriginal Australians

Q8 Which wind instrument was developed by Indigenous Australians?

    A Clarinet
    B Bassoon
    C Flute
    D Didgeridoo

Q9 Fletcher Christian led which mutiny?

    A The Potemkin Mutiny
    B The Hermione Mutiny
    C The Mutiny on the Bounty
    D The SS Columbia Eagle Mutiny

Q10 In what year did the first convicts arrive in Australia?

    A 1690
    B 1720
    C 1788
    D 1830

<u>**Australia 2 (average)**</u>

Q1 Who was the first person to circumnavigate Australia?

Q2 In what year did the Federation of Australia occur?

Q3 Arthur Phillip was the first Governor of which British colony?

Q4 What is Australia's national day of remembrance called, which is held on 25th April ever year?

Q5 What was the first campaign the Australian military participated in during the First World War?

Q6 Which Australian Prime Minister disappeared?

Q7 What houses is the Australian Parliament composed of?

Q8 Sydney Cove was named in honour of which British Home Secretary?

Q9 Van Diemen's Land was a name used by Europeans for which island?

Q10 The Australian frontier wars took place during how many centuries?

<u>**Australia 3 (expert)**</u>

Q1 Which political party won the largest number of seats in Australia's inaugural parliament?

Q2 Which fleet set sail in 1787 to create the first European settlement in Australia?

Q3 The Eureka Rebellion was instigated by what type of miners?

Q4 *Terra nullius* is a Latin term meaning what?

Q5 What date is Australia Day held on?

Q6 Pemulwuy was a member of what clan?

Q7 Which patron of the natural sciences took part in James Cook's first voyage (1768-71)?

Q8 Which port is the site of the first European settlement in Australia?

Q9 Which island was Thursday October Christian I born on?

Q10 In what years did the Caledon Bay crisis occur?

<u>**China 1 (easy)**</u>

Q1 Which emperor ordered the creation of the Terracotta Army?

   A Qin Er Shi
   B Qin Shi Huang
   C Ziying
   D Wu of Han

Q2 What was the main media for writing documents in China prior to the introduction of paper in the first and second centuries AD?

   A Stone
   B Papyrus
   C Bamboo slips
   D Quipu

Q3 The Republic of China is now confined to which island?

   A Tahiti
   B Taiwan
   C Oahu
   D Viti Levu

Q4 Where did Chinese students build a Goddess of Democracy in May 1989?

   A Summer Palace
   B Tiananmen Square
   C Temple of Heaven
   D Jiuzhaigou

Q5 How old was Puyi when he abdicated in 1912?

   A 2
   B 6
   C 19
   D 54

Q6 Yuan Shikai became President of what in 1912?

    A Republic of China
    B People's Republic of China
    C Kingdom of China
    D Hong Kong

Q7 The Warlord Era took place in what century?

    A 14th
    B 17th
    C 19th
    D 20th

Q8 Chiang Kai-shek died on what island?

    A Tasmania
    B Madagascar
    C Taiwan
    D Honshu

Q9 The Mandate of Heaven was used since ancient times to justify what?

    A Expansionism
    B Material inequality
    C Religious persecution
    D The rule of the Emperor of China

Q10 Giant Wild Goose Pagoda is located in which Chinese province?

    A Shaanxi
    B Guangdong
    C Zhejiang
    D Shandong

<u>**China 2 (average)**</u>

Q1 In Chou Dynasty culture, what shape was the world represented as?

Q2 Confucius was a philosopher from which period of Chinese history?

Q3 The majority of the existing Great Wall of China is from which dynasty?

Q4 The Boxer Rebellion occurred during which dynasty?

Q5 In what year did Hong Kong formally change hands, from the United Kingdom to the People's Republic of China?

Q6 Which campaign, from 1958 to 1962, aimed to rapidly transform China from an agrarian economy into a socialist society through rapid industrialization and collectivization?

Q7 The Xinhai Revolution resulted in the abdication of which Emperor?

Q8 Who are China's (and in turn the world's) largest ethnic group?

Q9 Who was the founder and leader of the Taiping Heavenly Kingdom?

Q10 Zhang Zuolin was the Warlord of which region of China?

<u>**China 3 (expert)**</u>

Q1 What four symbols represent the four seasons, as well as north, south, east and west?

Q2 What was the occupation of Ku K'ai-chih?

Q3 Zhu Yuanzhang was better known by what name?

Q4 Hong Taiji (also referred to as Abahai) was a member of which ethnic group?

Q5 The Emperor K'ang-hsi ruled for how many years?

Q6 The Manchu prince Dorgon is known for forcing all Han Chinese men to wear their hair in what?

Q7 The Taiping Rebellion occurred in what years?

Q8 Which Chinese politician served as the Viceroy of Zhili, Huguang and Liangguang during the 19th century?

Q9 Empress Xiaoqinxian is buried in which imperial mausoleum complex?

Q10 Who wrote the *Records of the Grand Historian*?

Q1 What was the principal religion of the Gupta Empire?

    A Islam
    B Christianity
    C Hinduism
    D Buddhism

Q2 Who was assassinated by Nathuram Godse on 30th January 1948?

    A Surya Sen
    B Mahatma Gandhi
    C Batukeshwar Dutt
    D Bhupendra Kumar Datta

Q3 Who was the chief architect of the Taj Mahal?

    A Makramat Khan
    B Ustad Isa
    C Mir Abdul Karim
    D Ustad Ahmad Lahori

Q4 Qutb Minar is what type of structure?

    A Temple
    B Palace
    C Minaret
    D Castle

Q5 Who was Kabir a disciple of?

    A Vallabhacharya
    B Ramanuja
    C Ramananda
    D Madhvacharya

Q6 Which monument was not built by Shah Jahan?

A Taj Mahal
B Red Fort
C Jama Masjid
D Fatehpur Sikri

Q7 In what year was the first of the three Round Table Conferences held?

A 1889
B 1927
C 1930
D 1944

Q8 Presidency University is based in which Indian city?

A Bengaluru
B Kolkata
C Mumbai
D New Delhi

Q9 As well as England and France, which other country had an East India Company?

A Spain
B The Netherlands
C Austria
D Russia

Q10 In which centuries did the Bengali renaissance occur?

A 16th and 17th
B 17th and 18th
C 18th and 19th
D 19th and 20th

India 2 (average)

Q1 The Kushan king Kanishka encouraged the spread of which religion?

Q2 Who was the first President of India?

Q3 In what year was Goa captured by the Portuguese?

Q4 What political party was Mahatma Gandhi a member of?

Q5 Who is known as the Napoleon of India?

Q6 What dynasty was ruing northern India when Alexander the Great invaded?

Q7 The National Song of India, *Vande Mataram*, was published in which 1882 novel?

Q8 Dayananda Saraswati founded what Hindu reform movement in 1875?

Q9 Who was the founder of the Vijayanagara Empire?

Q10 Bakht Khan was commander-in-chief of Indian forces during which conflict?

<u>**India 3 (expert)**</u>

Q1 Who was the first Governor-General of Bengal?

Q2 Who fought at the Second Battle of Panipat?

Q3 Mahesh Das was better known by what name?

Q4 Who is the 'doctrine of lapse' policy most commonly associated with?

Q5 Who founded Agra in 1504?

Q6 Who was the first Mughal emperor to enforce Sharia law in India?

Q7 The first Sanskrit grammar book *Ashtadhyayi* was written by who?

Q8 The Ellora Caves feature monuments to which three religions?

Q9 Which three empires did the Tripartite Struggle occur between?

Q10 In what century did work start on the Buddhist complex, Sanchi?

<u>**Japan 1 (easy)**</u>

Q1 In what century did Emperor Jimmu come to power?

    A 6th century BC
    B 7th century BC
    C 2nd century BC
    D 3rd century AD

Q2 Buddhism and which other religion are Japan's two main religions?

    A Shinto
    B Taoism
    C Christianity
    D Hinduism

Q3 The first Europeans to reach Japan were from what country?

    A Spain
    B Portugal
    C England
    D USA

Q4 Hirohito was emperor of Japan during which war?

    A Russo-Japanese War
    B First Sino-Japanese War
    C World War One
    D World War Two

Q5 Where was the Battle of Dan-no-ura fought?

    A On a field
    B On a mountain
    C At sea
    D In the air

Q6 Which Dutch monarch urged Japan to open up?

    A Beatrix
    B William II
    C William-Alexander
    D Wilhelmina

Q7 A *kimono* is what kind of clothing?

    A Skirt
    B Dress
    C Gloves
    D Hat

Q8 A *koto* is what kind of musical instrument?

    A Stringed
    B Woodwind
    C Brass
    D Drum

Q9 What was the Imperial capital of Japan prior to Tokyo?

    A Nagasaki
    B Hiroshima
    C Kyoto
    D Osaka

Q10 In which period of Japanese history was the country Westernised?

    A Nara period
    B Heian period
    C Edo period
    D Meiji period

<u>**Japan 2 (average)**</u>

Q1 Seppuku, part of the code of Samurai warriors, is better known by what name?

Q2 What was the former name of Tokyo?

Q3 Who was the military dictator of Japan during the period from 1185 to 1868 (with exceptions)?

Q4 Which national holiday celebrates the mythological foundation of Japan and the accession of its first emperor?

Q5 The 'Black Ships' refers to the arrival of Western vessels in Japan in which two centuries?

Q6 Sakoku was what kind of foreign policy?

Q7 Osaka Castle was constructed during which century?

Q8 During the Nanboku-chō period, was the Southern Court or the Northern Court the 'senior imperial line'?

Q9 Who was the first Englishman to reach Japan?

Q10 What is the oldest recorded name of Japan?

<u>Japan 3 (expert)</u>

Q1 What is the name of the period in Japanese history between 14,000–300 BCE where it was inhabited by a hunter-gatherer culture?

Q2 The Genpei War was a civil war fought between which two clans?

Q3 In which period of Japanese history was Chinese influence at its height?

Q4 In what year did the US Navy sail four ships into the bay at Edo, threatening war if Japan did not begin trade with the West?

Q5 What is the oldest extant chronicle in Japan?

Q6 The Fujiwara clan descended from which other clan?

Q7 The Bell of Nanbanji was made in which country?

Q8 Hokki-ji temple was built at the end of which period?

Q9 What was Tadao Ando's occupation?

Q10 The martial arts kenjutsu, kendo, kyūdō, sōjutsu, jujutsu, and sumo were all established during which period?

Q1 Which tsar founded St Petersburg in 1703?

    A Catherine the Great
    B Ivan the Terrible
    C Peter the Great
    D Alexander I

Q2 Which tsar was assassinated in 1881?

    A Alexander I
    B Alexander II
    C Nicholas II
    D Michael

Q3 How many revolutions were there following the abdication of Nicholas II?

    A 1
    B 2
    C 3
    D 4

Q4 The Winter Palace is a former royal residence in which city?

    A Kazan
    B Moscow
    C Vladivostok
    D St Petersburg

Q5 Who were Russia's three main opponents in the Crimean War?

    A Britain, France and Germany
    B Britain, France and the Ottoman Empire
    C France, Spain and the Ottoman Empire
    D Spain, Portugal and the Ottoman Empire

Q6 Who became the first Prime Minister of Russia in 1905?

A Sergei Witte
B Ivan Goremykin
C Ivan Durnovo
D Boris Stürmer

Q7 Mikhail Gorbachev formally resigned as President of the USSR on Christmas day of what year?

A 1989
B 1990
C 1991
D 1992

Q8 Who launched the Massacre of Novgorod?

A Catherine the Great
B Peter the Great
C Ivan the Terrible
D Alexander III

Q9 During which century did Moscow emerge as the dominant Russian principality?

A 1st century
B 5th century
C 14th century
D 17th century

Q10 What shape are the domes on Russian Orthodox churches?

A Square
B Onion
C Pyramid
D Spherical

<u>**Russia 2 (average)**</u>

Q1 What was the last royal dynasty to rule Russia?

Q2 Bloody Sunday occurred in what year?

Q3 What does USSR stand for?

Q4 Who was the first Romanov ruler of Russia?

Q5 Simbirsk was the childhood home of which two revolutionaries?

Q6 The Catherine Palace and Alexander Palace are located in which Russian town?

Q7 In which Siberian town was Grigori Rasputin born?

Q8 Who became the first President of Russia after the Dissolution of the Soviet Union?

Q9 The Russian Constitution of 1906 was enacted on the eve of the opening of what?

Q10 Who was the first Tatar Tsar of Russia?

Russia 3 (expert)

Q1 Where were Nicholas II and his family murdered in 1918?

Q2 In what year was serfdom abolished in Russia?

Q3 What office did Vyacheslav von Plehve hold when he was assassinated in 1904?

Q4 Vice-Admiral Stepan Makarov died during which war?

Q5 The USSR was separated into how many countries in 1991?

Q6 Mikhail Kalashnikov developed which assault rifle?

Q7 What was a *moujik*?

Q8 Alexander Nevsky agreed to pay tribute to which khanate?

Q9 Andrei Rublev is considered one of the best Russians in which field?

Q10 Which Russian prevented nuclear war during the 1983 Soviet nuclear false alarm incident?

<u>**Scandinavia 1 (easy)**</u>

Q1 Before becoming part of Germany, which country controlled Schleswig-Holstein?

    A Sweden
    B Denmark
    C Poland
    D Belgium

Q2 Gustavus Adolphus ruled which country?

    A Denmark
    B Norway
    C Finland
    D Sweden

Q3 Research suggests that ice skating was invented in which present-day country?

    A Norway
    B Iceland
    C Sweden
    D Finland

Q4 What term defines Ahrensburg culture?

    A Mercantile
    B Hunter-gatherer
    C Settled farming
    D Mercenary

Q5 What is a *lavvu*?

    A Temporary dwelling
    B Village
    C Canoe
    D Sleigh

Q6 The 'stone ship' was an early custom in what?

A Coronations
B Warfare
C Burials
D Sailing

Q7 Harald Hardrada was slain in battle in which kingdom?

A Kingdom of Norway
B Kingdom of France
C Kingdom of England
D Kingdom of Denmark

Q8 In Norse mythology people who die in what go to Valhalla?

A The sea
B Battle
C Norway
D Their sleep

Q9 Which Nordic country is governed by the Althing, the oldest parliament in the world?

A Iceland
B Finland
C Norway
D Denmark

Q10 How many people called Christian have been King of Denmark?

A 0
B 1
C 4
D 10

Scandinavia 2 (average)

Q1 Which Swedish Prime Minister was assassinated in 1986?

Q2 The Battle of Poltava was fought between Sweden and which other country?

Q3 Finnish President Kyösti Kallio was a member of what political party?

Q4 The Sámi people inhabit how many Nordic countries?

Q5 The Alvastra pile-dwelling is located in what country?

Q6 Which king introduced Christianity to Denmark?

Q7 What was the name of the union that joined the Kingdoms of Denmark, Norway and Sweden under one monarch in 1397?

Q8 The Treaty of Nystad was the last peace treaty of what war?

Q9 Who is said to have founded the first Norse settlement in Greenland?

Q10 The Gunboat War was fought between Denmark-Norway and which other country?

<u>**Scandinavia 3 (expert)**</u>

Q1 Which Danish nobleman and astronomer was granted the island of Hven by King Frederick II?

Q2 Axel Oxenstierna held which position in the Swedish government between 1612 and 1654?

Q3 The Vendel Period precedes which period of Swedish history?

Q4 The Golden Horns of Gallehus date from which century?

Q5 Which Norwegian king founded the city of Trondheim?

Q6 What was a *völva* in the Old Norse religion?

Q7 In what year was the title Archbishop of Uppsala established?

Q8 What was the name of the war waged between Finland and the Soviet Union between 1939 and 1940?

Q9 What intergovernmental organisation was founded in 1952?

Q10 Who headed the government of Norway during its occupation by the Nazis?

Latin America 1 (easy)

Q1 The Treaty of Tordesillas was signed between which two countries?

    A Portugal and the Crown of Castile (Spain)
    B France and the Crown of Castile (Spain)
    C Britain and Portugal
    D Portugal and the Netherlands

Q2 Which of the following countries speaks Portuguese?

    A Uruguay
    B Brazil
    C Argentina
    D Peru

Q3 Who was King of Portugal during the Brazilian War of Independence?

    A Alfonso I
    B Manuel I
    C John III
    D John VI

Q4 José de San Martín served as Protector of which country?

    A Venezuela
    B Bolivia
    C Peru
    D Columbia

Q5 What type of mining is Potosí known for?

    A Salt
    B Coal
    C Silver
    D Gold

Q6 Who served as the first President of Mexico?

    A Guadalupe Victoria
    B Enrique Peña Nieto
    C Manuel González Flores
    D Pancho Villa

Q7 In which war did Mexico lose approximately half of its territory?

    A Mexican-American War
    B First World War
    C Texas Revolution
    D Apache–Mexico Wars

Q8 How many times did Ramón Castilla serve as President of Peru?

    A 0
    B 1
    C 3
    D 5

Q9 In parts of South America a 'gaucho' was skilled at what?

    A Writing
    B Construction
    C Horse riding
    D Mining

Q10 The mercenary William Walker, who briefly served as President of Nicaragua, was from which country?

    A Nicaragua
    B Mexico
    C United Kingdom
    D USA

Q1 The Declaration of Independence of the Mexican Empire was issued in what year?

Q2 Who was the first ruler of the Empire of Brazil?

Q3 The term Libertadores refers to the principal leaders of which wars of independence?

Q4 The Primera Junta was the first independent government of which country?

Q5 The Battle of Ayacucho was fought in which war?

Q6 Antonio José de Sucre served as President of which two countries?

Q7 Colonel Cândido Rondon and which US President took part in an expedition in Brazil between 1913 and 1914?

Q8 The revolutionary Pancho Villa briefly served as Governor of which Mexican state?

Q9 Which European ruler attempted to turn Mexico into a puppet state in the 1860s?

Q10 The Caste War of Yucatán involved which group rebelling against the European-descended population of Mexico?

Latin America 3 (expert)

Q1 Gran Colombia included parts of which present-day countries?

Q2 In which city did the May Revolution (1810) occur?

Q3 The Confederation of the Equator (a short-lived rebellion against the newly independent Empire of Brazil) took place in what year?

Q4 The Chilean War of Independence is traditionally divided into what three stages?

Q5 Simón Bolívar played a key role in the establishment of which state that endured from 1819 to 1831?

Q6 Who was President of Chile when the Chilean Civil War of 1891 broke out?

Q7 In what year was the President of Argentina, Miguel Ángel Juárez Celman, deposed?

Q8 Which five countries were formerly part of the Federal Republic of Central America?

Q9 During the civil wars that followed Argentina's declaration of independence, who were the Federalists opposed to?

Q10 What was the nickname of the Argentine politician and army officer Juan Manuel de Rosas?

Q1 What name was given to the women who campaigned to have the vote in the first two decades of the 20th century?

    A Anarchists
    B Suffragettes
    C Peelites
    D Libertarians

Q2 Who is the national personification of the United Kingdom?

    A Uncle Sam
    B Deutscher Michel
    C John Bull
    D Helvetia

Q3 As well as England, which other part of the United Kingdom was originally part of the Kingdom of England?

    A Northern Ireland
    B Scotland
    C Wales
    D Shetland Islands

Q4 Who was the longest serving British Prime Minister of the 20th century?

    A Winston Churchill
    B Margaret Thatcher
    C Stanley Baldwin
    D Herbert Henry Asquith

Q5 In what year did the United Kingdom join the European Economic Community?

    A 1919
    B 1945
    C 1973
    D 1982

Q6 Which royal house were the Jacobites loyal to?

    A Blois
    B Tudor
    C Windsor
    D Stuart

Q7 The National Health Service was established in the aftermath of which war?

    A Crimean War
    B First World War
    C Second World War
    D Gulf War

Q8 At its peak, approximately how much of the Earth's land area did the British Empire cover?

    A 10%
    B 15%
    C 25%
    D 40%

Q9 What is the United Kingdom's oldest commercial television network?

    A BBC (British Broadcasting Corporation)
    B ITV (Independent Television)
    C Channel 4
    D Channel 5

Q10 Who was the first Jewish British Prime Minister?

    A Henry Addington
    B Benjamin Disraeli
    C Henry John Temple, Viscount Palmerston
    D Harold Wilson

<u>**United Kingdom 2 (average)**</u>

Q1 Which soldier and statesman was Downing Street named after?

Q2 Which palace was the birthplace and ancestral home of Winston Churchill?

Q3 Which three national flags are featured on the Union Jack?

Q4 Interwar Britain was a period lasting between what years?

Q5 In what year did Parliament grant Wales, Scotland and Northern Ireland devolved government?

Q6 Which Prime Minister led the United Kingdom to victory in the First World War?

Q7 What was the occupation of John Maynard Keynes?

Q8 In which city did the Peterloo Massacre occur?

Q9 The sunburst flag was associated with nationalism in which country?

Q10 Which renowned English film director was born in Essex in 1899?

<u>**United Kingdom 3 (expert)**</u>

Q1 How old was William Pitt the Younger when he first attended Pembroke College, Cambridge?

Q2 What was the first submarine commissioned by the Royal Navy?

Q3 Which mathematician cracked German codes at Bletchley Park during the Second World War?

Q4 Which suffragette died after being hit by George V's horse at the 1913 Derby?

Q5 In what year was the Irish Free State established?

Q6 Which incident in 1861 threatened war between the United Kingdom and the USA?

Q7 The Midlothian campaign refers to a series of foreign policy speeches given by which British Prime Minister?

Q8 Which revolutionary organisation was founded in 1858?

Q9 Who were the two founders of *Punch* magazine?

Q10 'The Ashes' test cricket series originates from an Australian victory in what year?

Q1 Which Apollo mission landed man on the moon for the first time?

A Apollo 10
B Apollo 11
C Apollo 12
D Apollo 13

Q2 'In God We Trust' is the motto of the USA and which state?

A Alabama
B Florida
C Georgia
D Oklahoma

Q3 How many colonies rebelled to form the USA?

A 5
B 10
C 13
D 15

Q4 Who was the only person to become vice president and president after successive resignations?

A Richard Nixon
B Harry Truman
C Gerald Ford
D Warren Harding

Q5 The Alamo is located in which city?

A Houston
B Austin
C San Antonio
D San Diego

Q6 The United States Military Academy, better known as West Point, is located in which US state?

    A New York
    B New Jersey
    C Virginia
    D South Carolina

Q7 Which president's re-election campaign included the slogan 'He kept us out of the war'?

    A Franklin Roosevelt
    B Abraham Lincoln
    C Woodrow Wilson
    D George H W Bush

Q8 The Great Society was a set of domestic programs launched by which president?

    A Franklin Roosevelt
    B Dwight Eisenhower
    C John F Kennedy
    D Lyndon Johnson

Q9 Which US State was the first to be admitted to the Union?

    A Massachusetts
    B New York
    C Delaware
    D New Hampshire

Q10 How many times was Franklin Roosevelt elected President of the USA?

    A 2
    B 3
    C 4
    D 5

<u>**USA 2 (average)**</u>

Q1 In what year was the Transcontinental Railroad completed?

Q2 Which American political protest took place on December 16ᵗʰ 1773?

Q3 What was New York called prior to 1664?

Q4 Woodrow Wilson embarked on a tour around the USA in 1919 to promote the country's entry into which international organisation?

Q5 Which US state has held the most nuclear tests?

Q6 Which four presidents are featured on Mount Rushmore?

Q7 Who was King of Great Britain when revolution broke out in the North American colonies?

Q8 How many of the USA's first five presidents were natives of Virginia?

Q9 Who is the longest serving Chief Justice in the history of the United States Supreme Court?

Q10 What do the stripes represent on the USA's flag?

<u>**USA 3 (expert)**</u>

Q1 After which US president is the capital of Liberia named?

Q2 In what year was the Republic of Texas annexed by the USA?

Q3 The activities of which pirates prompted the establishment of the United States Navy?

Q4 Daniel Boone is known for exploring and settling which future US state?

Q5 What is the Latin motto of the United States Army Special Forces?

Q6 Which armed uprising occurred in Massachusetts between 1786 and 1787?

Q7 What are the first ten amendments in the United States Constitution called?

Q8 'Arsenal of Democracy' was a slogan used by Franklin Roosevelt during a radio broadcast in what year?

Q9 Which country did the United States attempt to invade in the Bay of Pigs Invasion?

Q10 Which music festival was held in New York State from August 15th to August 18th 1969?

Politics

<u>**18th Century Politics 1 (easy)**</u>

Q1 Which two states gave land to create Washington D.C.?

    A Kentucky and Maryland
    B North Carolina and Virginia
    C Virginia and Maryland
    D New York and Virginia

Q2 Before its union with the English Parliament, how many legislative chambers did the Scottish Parliament have?

    A 1
    B 2
    C 3
    D 4

Q3 Frederick the Great ruled which kingdom?

    A Piedmont-Sardinia
    B Austria-Hungary
    C Prussia
    D Portugal

Q4 Who was Peter III of Russia's wife?

    A Maria Nagaya
    B Alexandra Feodorovna
    C Marie Antoinette
    D Catherine the Great

Q5 What did the Province of Upper Canada ban the importation of in 1793?

    A Whiskey
    B Furniture
    C Slaves
    D Timber

Q6 Which two countries were engaged in a Quasi-War between 1798 and 1800?

    A Britain and France
    B Britain and Spain
    C Britain and USA
    D France and USA

Q7 Which Russian Tsar is credited with Westernising Russia?

    A Ivan the Terrible
    B Feodor III
    C Peter the Great
    D Alexander I

Q8 Who was the first Governor of Virginia?

    A Benjamin Franklin
    B Alexander Hamilton
    C Aaron Burr
    D Patrick Henry

Q9 Pyotr Rumyantsev was Governor of what?

    A Ukraine
    B Crimea
    C Lithuania
    D Little Russia

Q10 The feminist Olympe de Gouges was from what country?

    A France
    B USA
    C Switzerland
    D Austria

<u>**18th Century Politics 2 (average)**</u>

Q1 William Pitt the Elder was leader of which political party?

Q2 Which British Prime Minister introduced income tax?

Q3 Who became King of Denmark in 1766?

Q4 What was the name of the peasant rebellion that took place in Russia between 1773 and 1775?

Q5 Who was the only female ruler of the Habsburg Monarchy?

Q6 Prithvi Narayan Shah was the first King of what?

Q7 Theobald Wolfe Tone was one of the founding members of which radical political organisation?

Q8 Gilbert du Motier, Marquis de Lafayette was a key figure in which two revolutions?

Q9 Túpac Amaru II led a revolution against the Spanish in what present-day country?

Q10 Francis II Rákóczi led an uprising against which monarchy?

<u>**18th Century Politics 3 (expert)**</u>

Q1 What did George Washington warn the American people about in his farewell address in 1796?

Q2 The Treaty of Aix-la-Chapelle ended which war?

Q3 Tadeusz Rejtan was a nobleman from which Commonwealth?

Q4 Which Portuguese king was nicknamed 'The Reformer'?

Q5 What is the name of the ancestral home of the Bonaparte family?

Q6 In what year was the Dutch East India Company dissolved?

Q7 Who founded the Bavarian Illuminati?

Q8 What ethnic group was the religious and military leader Sheikh Mansur associated with?

Q9 In what year did Toussaint Louverture become Governor-General of Saint-Domingue?

Q10 What title did Balaji Baji Rao hold?

<u>**19th Century Politics 1 (easy)**</u>

Q1 The United States acquired Louisiana Territory off which country in 1803?

    A United Kingdom
    B France
    C Spain
    D The Netherlands

Q2 How many terms did William Gladstone serve as prime minister of the United Kingdom?

    A 1
    B 2
    C 4
    D 5

Q3 Which empire was known as the 'Sick Man of Europe' during the nineteenth century?

    A French Empire
    B Ottoman Empire
    C Spanish Empire
    D British Empire

Q4 The Risorgimento resulted in the unification of which country?

    A Spain
    B Belgium
    C Germany
    D Italy

Q5 How many Democrats served as President of the United States during the Gilded Age?

    A 0
    B 1
    C 3
    D 4

Q6 William Wilberforce is commonly associated with which political movement?

   A Suffragettes
   B Abolitionism
   C Progressivism
   D Toryism

Q7 José Rizal was executed during which revolution?

   A French Revolution
   B Philippine Revolution
   C Argentine Revolution
   D Mexican Revolution

Q8 Who founded the Austrian Empire in 1804?

   A Archduke Franz Ferdinand of Austria
   B Napoleon Bonaparte
   C Francis II, Holy Roman Emperor
   D Kaiser Wilhelm I of Germany

Q9 The American Colonization Society is associated with which African country?

   A Liberia
   B Chad
   C Ivory Coast
   D Burkina Faso

Q10 In what year was the *Communist Manifesto* published?

   A 1815
   B 1848
   C 1888
   D 1917

Q1 Which British prime minister was assassinated in 1812?

Q2 In what year was slavery abolished throughout the British Empire?

Q3 Northern Democrats who supported an immediate peace treaty with the Confederate States of America were commonly called what?

Q4 Who became the first King of Italy in 1861?

Q5 Napoleon III fell from power after which war?

Q6 Which Conservative Home Secretary, who later became Prime Minister, is responsible for introduction of the Metropolitan Police Act of 1829?

Q7 The Reform Act of 1867 enfranchised which group of people in England and Wales for the first time?

Q8 The British Whig Party merged into which political party in 1859?

Q9 Which kingdoms were formally merged in 1801?

Q10 The Great Game was a diplomatic confrontation between which two empires?

<u>**19th Century Politics 3 (expert)**</u>

Q1 Who was vice president of the Confederate States of America?

Q2 Who was the first Jew to be elected to the United States Senate in 1853?

Q3 Chartism was a working class movement for political reform in which country?

Q4 Which 1802 treaty temporarily ended hostilities between France and the United Kingdom during the Napoleonic Wars?

Q5 Which Japanese policy was formally ended in 1854?

Q6 What was the name of the open letter that was issued by Pope Leo XIII in 1891, addressing the condition of the working classes?

Q7 Nikola Karev was a revolutionary leader in which present-day country?

Q8 Kamehameha I ruled which kingdom?

Q9 Which city was attacked by some 200 incendiary balloons in 1849?

Q10 Which Muslim revolt occurred in China between 1862 and 1877?

<u>**20th Century Politics 1 (easy)**</u>

Q1 'I like Ike' was a slogan used in whose presidential campaign?

    A Ronald Reagan
    B John F Kennedy
    C William McKinley
    D Dwight Eisenhower

Q2 Which President of the United States is said to have worked only 4 hours a day?

    A Calvin Coolidge
    B Herbert Hoover
    C Gerald Ford
    D Andrew Jackson

Q3 Who served as Deputy Prime Minister of the United Kingdom during the Second World War?

    A Neville Chamberlain
    B Edward Heath
    C Clement Atlee
    D Herbert Henry Asquith

Q4 The 'Iron Curtain' was the name of a boundary between two power blocs on which continent?

    A Europe
    B Africa
    C Asia
    D South America

Q5 Who was the first female Prime Minister of the United Kingdom?

    A Theresa May
    B Amber Rudd
    C Margaret Thatcher
    D Nancy Astor

Q6 Which international organisation did the United Nations replace?

    A NATO
    B The Warsaw Pact
    C The World Bank
    D The League of Nations

Q7 The Khmer Rouge was a name for the Communist regime that ruled which country between 1975 and 1979?

    A Vietnam
    B Laos
    C Cambodia
    D Thailand

Q8 The October Crisis (1970) occurred in which Canadian province?

    A Alberta
    B Manitoba
    C Ontario
    D Quebec

Q9 The *Estado Novo* was an authoritarian regime that governed which country between 1933 and 1974?

    A Spain
    B Portugal
    C Italy
    D Morocco

Q10 Who was Prime Minister of Canada during the Second World War?

    A Justin Trudeau
    B Pierre Trudeau
    C William Lyon Mackenzie King
    D Wilfrid Laurier

<u>**20th Century Politics 2 (average)**</u>

Q1 Which amendment to the United States Constitution established prohibition?

Q2 Who was President of the United States when the 1929 Wall Street Crash occurred?

Q3 By what name is the German government between the end of World War One and the rise of Adolf Hitler referred to?

Q4 Who was the leader of Free France during World War Two?

Q5 Who was president of South Vietnam before his overthrow and murder in 1963?

Q6 The Black Hundreds were an ultra-nationalist group in which country?

Q7 Which political party was Nelson Mandela a member of?

Q8 Who did Iranian militants want returned in exchange for US hostages in 1979?

Q9 Eugene V. Debs was a US presidential candidate for which political party?

Q10 In which city was the League of Nations headquartered?

<u>**20th Century Politics 3 (expert)**</u>

Q1 Edward VIII of the United Kingdom abdicated in 1936 to marry which American?

Q2 The Harvester Judgement was a benchmark legal case for ensuring workers in which country were paid a fair basic wage?

Q3 In what year did Israel become a nation?

Q4 Who was the first Secretary-General of the United Nations?

Q5 Which British dominion became a province of Canada in 1949?

Q6 Fulgencio Batista was overthrown as the leader of which country in 1959?

Q7 The Republic of Macedonia became a member of the United Nations in 1993 under what name?

Q8 In what year did the North American Free Trade Agreement come into force?

Q9 Who became President of Brazil after a coup in 1930?

Q10 What does Mustafa Kemal Atatürk's surname mean?

Answers

Answers: General History

General History 1 (easy)

Q1 Guillotined
Q2 Iberian
Q3 Asia, Africa and Europe
Q4 Huns
Q5 Prague
Q6 London Underground
Q7 Max Weber
Q8 Saint Petersburg
Q9 2
Q10 Republic of Texas

General History 2 (easy)

Q1 Greece
Q2 Reims Cathedral
Q3 Winston Churchill, Joseph Stalin and Franklin Roosevelt
Q4 Napoleon I
Q5 Ruler
Q6 Chicago
Q7 First
Q8 France
Q9 Kaiser Wilhelm II of Germany
Q10 South Africa

General History 3 (easy)

Q1 Charles Lindbergh
Q2 Mecca
Q3 Argentina
Q4 USA
Q5 Italy
Q6 Pirates
Q7 Gravesend, England
Q8 Immigrant inspection station

Q9 London
Q10 Lisbon

General History 4 (easy)

Q1 Charles Wilkes Booth
Q2 Christianity
Q3 Farmers
Q4 Abraham Lincoln
Q5 Australasia and Antarctica
Q6 Sarajevo
Q7 Henry II
Q8 Baltimore
Q9 Apple
Q10 The Americas

General History 5 (easy)

Q1 Herodotus
Q2 Portugal
Q3 Britain and China
Q4 Battle of the Little Bighorn
Q5 Hawaiian Islands
Q6 Louis XIV
Q7 Horses
Q8 Heart
Q9 Islam
Q10 1910's

General History 6 (easy)

Q1 Christopher Wren
Q2 Wimbledon
Q3 Watergate Scandal
Q4 Argentina
Q5 Scotland
Q6 War of 1812
Q7 England

Q8 Iran

Q9 Holbeche House

Q10 French Indochina

General History 7 (easy)

Q1 Africa

Q2 15th

Q3 War of Spanish Succession

Q4 CNN

Q5 Russia

Q6 Calvin Coolidge

Q7 Finland

Q8 Zulus

Q9 England

Q10 Firing squad

General History 8 (easy)

Q1 Tudor

Q2 Achaemenid

Q3 Patrick Henry

Q4 Vikings

Q5 Asia

Q6 China

Q7 Harriet Beecher Stowe

Q8 Ottoman Empire

Q9 David Ben-Gurion

Q10 Aircraft

General History 9 (easy)

Q1 Adolf Hitler

Q2 Homer

Q3 Martin Luther King Jr.

Q4 Ship

Q5 Virginia

Q6 Russian Empire

Q7 United Kingdom
Q8 5th century BC
Q9 The Netherlands
Q10 1872

General History 10 (easy)

Q1 Archduke Franz Ferdinand
Q2 Saint Patrick
Q3 Military
Q4 Hellenistic Period
Q5 Plymouth
Q6 The Netherlands
Q7 Utah
Q8 Theodore Roosevelt
Q9 Japan
Q10 Royal Air Force

General History 11 (easy)

Q1 Brigham Young
Q2 The Netherlands
Q3 15th
Q4 Quebec City
Q5 Portable toilet
Q6 Mexico City
Q7 United Kingdom
Q8 Mexican-American War
Q9 Lake Placid 1980
Q10 Mustafa Kemal Atatürk

General History 12 (easy)

Q1 The Forum
Q2 France
Q3 Pearl Harbour
Q4 Crimean War
Q5 Charlemagne

Q6 Skopje
Q7 Sir Walter Raleigh
Q8 Memphis
Q9 World War 1
Q10 Inca Empire

General History 13 (easy)

Q1 London
Q2 An emperor
Q3 Paris
Q4 Dante Alighieri
Q5 Massachusetts Bay Colony
Q6 Lollardy
Q7 USA
Q8 Christian X of Denmark
Q9 Hall of Mirrors
Q10 Earthquake

General History 14 (easy)

Q1 White Star Line
Q2 World War One
Q3 Mongol Empire
Q4 Protestant
Q5 Pennsylvania
Q6 Hispaniola
Q7 Empire of Japan
Q8 Influenza
Q9 Philippines
Q10 Piggly Wiggly

General History 15 (easy)

Q1 Leif Erikson
Q2 Mosque
Q3 Andrew Johnson
Q4 Canada

Q5 Khmer Empire

Q6 Texas Longhorn

Q7 German Papiermark

Q8 Moscow

Q9 The Netherlands

Q10 John Profumo

General History 16 (easy)

Q1 Norwegian

Q2 Louis XIV

Q3 Cambodia

Q4 Finland

Q5 Jerusalem

Q6 India

Q7 Prague Spring

Q8 26 million

Q9 Fighter pilot

Q10 Wolf's Lair

General History 17 (easy)

Q1 4

Q2 Republic of Florence

Q3 Reconstruction

Q4 The Netherlands

Q5 Lawrence of Arabia

Q6 Communism

Q7 Munich

Q8 Russian Empire

Q9 Egypt

Q10 The Holocaust

General History 18 (easy)

Q1 *Queen Anne's Revenge*

Q2 Dominican

Q3 Republican

Q4 Cambodia

Q5 Argentina

Q6 The Great Purge

Q7 Saudi Arabia

Q8 Czechoslovakia

Q9 Soviet Union

Q10 Wisconsin

General History 19 (easy)

Q1 Yugoslavia

Q2 Duke of Lancaster

Q3 Atlantic

Q4 South America

Q5 Desiderius Erasmus

Q6 Banking

Q7 1946

Q8 Joseph Stalin

Q9 5

Q10 Brazil

General History 20 (easy)

Q1 Lancaster

Q2 Tunisia

Q3 Oxford

Q4 Mongolia

Q5 Catholic

Q6 1854

Q7 Ottoman Empire

Q8 Mexico

Q9 Hitler Youth

Q10 Franklin Roosevelt

General History 21 (average)

Q1 Whitechapel

Q2 Otto von Bismarck

Q3 Iceni

Q4 Portugal

Q5 Justinian

Q6 Robert Baden-Powell

Q7 Samuel Pepys

Q8 Florence

Q9 Ptolemy I Soter

Q10 *The Times*

General History 22 (average)

Q1 Queen Anne

Q2 Connecticut

Q3 Mary Queen of Scots

Q4 Julius and Ethel

Q5 Sudan

Q6 Memphis

Q7 The White House

Q8 English Heritage

Q9 Julius Caesar

Q10 Ivan the Terrible

General History 23 (average)

Q1 *The History of the Decline and Fall of the Roman Empire*

Q2 University of Bologna

Q3 Alexander Fleming

Q4 1945

Q5 Mercia and Powys

Q6 Catholic Church and Orthodox Church

Q7 Religious power

Q8 Giovanni Boccaccio

Q9 William I

Q10 The Pope

<u>General History 24 (average)</u>

Q1 Hengist and Horsa
Q2 Roman and Sasanian
Q3 Socrates
Q4 University of St Andrews
Q5 Nevada and Arizona
Q6 Holy Roman Emperor (Frederick I)
Q7 Bubonic, Septicemic and Pneumonic
Q8 Spanish Empire and Holy Roman Empire
Q9 Queen Isabella I of Castile and King Ferdinand II of Aragon
Q10 James Hargreaves

<u>General History 25 (average)</u>

Q1 North Side Gang
Q2 Russo-Japanese War (1904-05)
Q3 Bristol
Q4 Tiberius
Q5 American Revolutionary War
Q6 Encyclopaedia
Q7 13th-15th
Q8 Labour
Q9 Akkad
Q10 India

<u>General History 26 (average)</u>

Q1 Marxist
Q2 The Articles of Confederation
Q3 Southampton, England and New York City, USA
Q4 Humphry Davy
Q5 1901
Q6 Martha Washington
Q7 Niccolò Machiavelli
Q8 The Magnificent
Q9 German Renaissance
Q10 *Leviathan*

General History 27 (average)

Q1 July 4, 1776
Q2 Leopold II
Q3 New Jersey
Q4 Pancho Villa
Q5 Bournville
Q6 Twice as large
Q7 3
Q8 Protestant Reformation
Q9 The Habitation at Port-Royal
Q10 Tennessee

General History 28 (average)

Q1 The Lumière brothers
Q2 Pyramid of the Sun
Q3 Tutsi and Hutu
Q4 1947
Q5 Bonn
Q6 1814
Q7 Saint Alban
Q8 Philippe Pétain
Q9 The Three Wise Men
Q10 Louis XIV of France

General History 29 (average)

Q1 Cuthbert Collingwood
Q2 Louis XIV
Q3 Carthage
Q4 Toussaint Louverture
Q5 Alexei Nikolaevich, Tsarevich of Russia
Q6 Yuri Gagarin
Q7 Plymouth
Q8 Inca Empire
Q9 Soviet Union
Q10 Tsar Nicholas II of Russia

General History 30 (average)

Q1 The Office of Strategic Services
Q2 Gaul
Q3 1896
Q4 Edward IV, Edward V and Richard III
Q5 Eleanor of Aquitaine
Q6 Easter Island
Q7 Robert Stephenson
Q8 Dominican Order
Q9 Brighton
Q10 Venice and Genoa

General History 31 (average)

Q1 England
Q2 No
Q3 Bartolomeu Dias
Q4 Julius Caesar
Q5 Constantinople
Q6 Sir Walter Raleigh
Q7 1922
Q8 Gaul
Q9 China
Q10 John I of Portugal

General History 32 (average)

Q1 Olympic class
Q2 Londinium
Q3 Order of Assassins
Q4 Andrew Johnson
Q5 James II
Q6 George Herman Ruth Jr
Q7 History
Q8 Stockton and Darlington Railway
Q9 Quebec City
Q10 Saint-Domingue

General History 33 (average)

Q1 Queen Mary
Q2 The Elephant Man
Q3 Theodore Roosevelt
Q4 Leopold I
Q5 John Stith Pemberton
Q6 Architect
Q7 Suffolk
Q8 Motor Neurone Disease
Q9 Tea clipper
Q10 French Indochina

General History 34 (average)

Q1 Pudding Lane
Q2 Ferdinand Magellan
Q3 Han Dynasty
Q4 Edmund Hillary
Q5 Gordon Howe
Q6 The Crystal Palace
Q7 Trombone
Q8 Switzerland
Q9 East India Company
Q10 Cato the Younger

General History 35 (average)

Q1 Robert Walpole
Q2 Grover Cleveland
Q3 Eastern Roman Empire (Byzantine Empire)
Q4 Edo Castle
Q5 The slave trade
Q6 Franz Joseph I of Austria
Q7 1823
Q8 1948
Q9 Gustavus Adolphus of Sweden (Gustav II)
Q10 12th century

General History 36 (expert)

Q1 Annales
Q2 1453
Q3 Illustrating
Q4 Varina Farms
Q5 Harland and Wolff
Q6 George Stephen
Q7 Viceroyalty of the Río de la Plata
Q8 Bear Flag Revolt
Q9 Amaterasu
Q10 The Chinese Workers' and Peasants' Red Army

General History 37 (expert)

Q1 Henry McCarty
Q2 Greco-Persian Wars
Q3 Damascus
Q4 Powhatan (or Wahunsenacawh)
Q5 1766
Q6 Shawnee
Q7 Latin America
Q8 Tōgō Heihachirō
Q9 Alfred Leete
Q10 Decadent movement

General History 38 (expert)

Q1 Richard Lawrence
Q2 Mani
Q3 Ferdinand von Zeppelin
Q4 Morocco
Q5 1895
Q6 Huguenots
Q7 The system of slavery in the southern states of the USA
Q8 Fresh water
Q9 Battle of Karnal
Q10 Albanian

General History 39 (expert)

Q1 HMS *Agamemnon*
Q2 Persepolis
Q3 Pennsylvania
Q4 Russian
Q5 Lono
Q6 Fabergé eggs
Q7 Grigori Rasputin
Q8 The Short
Q9 Kingdom of Hungary
Q10 Society of Jesus (Jesuits)

General History 40 (expert)

Q1 Minoan
Q2 Douglas Hyde
Q3 War of Spanish Succession
Q4 Tsaritsa Alexandra Fyodorovna
Q5 USS *Maine*
Q6 Tengrism
Q7 Henry VI
Q8 Great Western Railway
Q9 Royal council (or King's court)
Q10 Photographer

General History 41 (expert)

Q1 Zoroastrianism
Q2 James IV
Q3 Unsinkable Mrs Brown
Q4 Monte Cassino
Q5 7
Q6 University of Padua
Q7 Kingdom of Scotland
Q8 1885
Q9 Upton Sinclair

Q10 David Lloyd George (UK), Woodrow Wilson (USA), Georges Clemenceau (France), and Vittorio Emanuele Orlando (Italy)

General History 42 (expert)

Q1 1869
Q2 Antonine Wall
Q3 The Rocket
Q4 Pius VI
Q5 Timur
Q6 *Rule of Saint Benedict*
Q7 1909
Q8 Duchy of Milan
Q9 Dutch Golden Age
Q10 Atahualpa, *Sapa Inca*

General History 43 (expert)

Q1 Peloponnesian War
Q2 1096
Q3 Battle of Culloden
Q4 United Kingdom and Iceland
Q5 Sirimavo Bandaranaike (Prime Minister of Sri Lanka)
Q6 Austro-Hungarian Empire
Q7 Eastern Roman Empire (Byzantine Empire)
Q8 Cossacks
Q9 Sam Houston
Q10 Edgar the Peaceful

General History 44 (expert)

Q1 Olympic Games, Pythian Games, Nemean Games and Isthmian Games
Q2 Emesa
Q3 Colossus of Rhodes, Great Pyramid of Giza, Hanging Gardens of Babylon, Lighthouse of Alexandria, Mausoleum at Halicarnassus, Statue of Zeus at Olympia and the Temple of Artemis at Ephesus
Q4 East India Company
Q5 Ellen Church

Q6 Bridge of his nose

Q7 Equites

Q8 Prince Shōtoku

Q9 Giovanni Pico della Mirandola

Q10 Charles George Gordon

General History 45 (expert)

Q1 Lexington Hotel

Q2 Gupta

Q3 Russo-Japanese War

Q4 Edith of Wessex

Q5 Gustavus Adolphus of Sweden (Gustav II)

Q6 Louis-Joseph de Montcalm

Q7 Boxers

Q8 Cape Colony

Q9 Standard Oil Company

Q10 Matthew Flinders

General History 46 (expert)

Q1 A golden age

Q2 1891-1916

Q3 12

Q4 Great auk

Q5 Russia

Q6 Temple of the Golden Pavilion

Q7 Witch hunter

Q8 Great Western Railway; London, Midland and Scottish Railway; London and North Eastern Railway; Southern Railway

Q9 Portugal

Q10 China

General History 47 (expert)

Q1 Leopold von Ranke

Q2 Sprung from Zeus's forehead, fully armed and bellowing her war cry

Q3 Francis Gary Powers

Q4 Gregory of Tours
Q5 George William Joy
Q6 *Guerra Grande*
Q7 1908
Q8 Porfirio Diaz Mori
Q9 The succession of an Emperor or Empress of India
Q10 Minister of the Interior

General History 48 (expert)

Q1 Mycenae
Q2 Yellow and Blue
Q3 1908
Q4 Seven Years' War
Q5 Nicola Sacco and Bartolomeo Vanzetti
Q6 The Butler Act
Q7 Fordlândia
Q8 Watergate scandal
Q9 Salvador Allende, President of Chile
Q10 Republic of Biafra

General History 49 (expert)

Q1 John Clem
Q2 Beehive tomb
Q3 El Salvador and Honduras
Q4 Merovech
Q5 Rollo
Q6 Sake Dean Mahomed
Q7 *Treatise on Tolerance*
Q8 Shah Jahan
Q9 House of Oldenburg
Q10 Tauride Palace

General History 50 (expert)

Q1 Emma Hamilton
Q2 Amerigo Vespucci

Q3 China
Q4 Marsilius of Padua
Q5 1274 and 1281
Q6 Noah
Q7 Queen Anne
Q8 The Second Opium War
Q9 Green beret
Q10 Anchor

Answers: Battles and Wars

Greco-Persian Wars 1 (easy)

Q1 Darius the Great
Q2 Battle of Marathon
Q3 A military commander
Q4 Sea
Q5 Mycale
Q6 Sparta
Q7 Peace of Callias
Q8 Infantry
Q9 Military formation
Q10 Sparta

Greco-Persian Wars 2 (average)

Q1 499 BC
Q2 Greek city states
Q3 Persian Empire
Q4 Xerxes I
Q5 Leonidas I, King of Sparta
Q6 The Delian League
Q7 The lower classes
Q8 Athens
Q9 The Wars of the Delian League
Q10 Cyprus

Greco-Persian Wars 3 (expert)

Q1 Aristagoras
Q2 Ionian Revolt
Q3 Artabanus of Persia
Q4 Cimon
Q5 Citizen soldiers
Q6 The Battle of Plataea
Q7 Cyrus the Younger
Q8 Athens and Eretria

Q9 Artaphernes
Q10 Athens

<u>The Punic Wars (average)</u>

Q1 Carthage
Q2 3
Q3 Second Punic War
Q4 Macedonian Wars
Q5 The Mediterranean
Q6 Hiero II of Syracuse
Q7 Carthage
Q8 Scipio Africanus
Q9 The Battle of Carthage
Q10 Third Punic War

<u>Norman Conquest 1 (easy)</u>

Q1 Edward the Confessor
Q2 Duke of Normandy
Q3 Domesday Book
Q4 Less than a year
Q5 English Channel
Q6 Normans
Q7 Eye
Q8 Anglo-Saxons
Q9 Kingdom of Norway
Q10 Brother

<u>Norman Conquest 2 (average)</u>

Q1 Harald Hardrada
Q2 The White Tower
Q3 Bayeux Tapestry
Q4 Stigand
Q5 Harald Hardrada
Q6 Senlac Hill
Q7 14th October

Q8 York

Q9 Eustace II, Count of Boulogne

Q10 The Vikings

Norman Conquest 3 (expert)

Q1 William of Poitiers

Q2 Waltham Abbey Church

Q3 West Midlands

Q4 24

Q5 Witenagemot

Q6 Militia

Q7 Waltheof, Earl of Northumbria

Q8 1068

Q9 1075

Q10 17th century

First Crusade 1 (easy)

Q1 1099

Q2 Urban II

Q3 Amiens

Q4 1096

Q5 Baldwin I

Q6 Antioch

Q7 7th

Q8 Kilij Arslan I

Q9 Seljuk Empire

Q10 Jews

First Crusade 2 (average)

Q1 God wills it

Q2 County of Edessa and Principality of Antioch

Q3 Alexios I Komnenos

Q4 Recover Jerusalem

Q5 Robert Curthose

Q6 The Tower of David

Q7 1096-99
Q8 Fatimid Caliphate
Q9 Baldwin I of Jerusalem
Q10 The East–West Schism

First Crusade 3 (expert)

Q1 Council of Clermont
Q2 1097
Q3 Cannibalism
Q4 Iftikhar al-Dawla
Q5 County of Tripoli
Q6 Merchant
Q7 Robert the Monk
Q8 The Crusade of 1101 (or the Crusade of the Faint-Hearted)
Q9 Walter the Penniless
Q10 Greek Orthodox

Third Crusade 1 (easy)

Q1 Ayyubid
Q2 Kingdom of Cyprus
Q3 Anatolian
Q4 Henry VI, Holy Roman Emperor
Q5 Fell out a window
Q6 Latin
Q7 Isaac II Angelos
Q8 1190
Q9 Italy
Q10 1190

Third Crusade 2 (average)

Q1 Leprosy
Q2 Philip II
Q3 Siege of Jerusalem (1187)
Q4 He drowned
Q5 Treaty of Jaffa

Q6 Richard I of England

Q7 Church of the Holy Sepulchre

Q8 Crusaders

Q9 Siege of Acre

Q10 Saladin

Third Crusade 3 (expert)

Q1 1187

Q2 Pope Gregory VIII

Q3 Baldwin of Forde

Q4 Grand Master of the Knights Templar

Q5 1189-91

Q6 Alys of France, Countess of Vexin

Q7 1191

Q8 Baldwin IV of Jerusalem

Q9 Dartmouth

Q10 Battle of Arsuf

Hundred Years' War 1 (easy)

Q1 116

Q2 5

Q3 Cousin

Q4 Battle of Agincourt

Q5 Joan of Arc

Q6 Longbow

Q7 Edward III

Q8 David II of Scotland

Q9 House of Valois

Q10 Treaty of London

Hundred Years' War 2 (average)

Q1 The right to rule the Kingdom of France

Q2 5

Q3 Edward III of England

Q4 Kingdom of France

Q5 Battle of Castillon

Q6 Henry V of England and Charles VI of France

Q7 Siege of Compiègne

Q8 Wars of the Roses

Q9 Black Death

Q10 Edward, the Black Prince

Hundred Years' War 3 (expert)

Q1 The Edwardian War (1337–1360), the Caroline War (1369–1389), and the Lancastrian War (1415–1453)

Q2 John Talbot, Earl of Shrewsbury

Q3 1429

Q4 Battle of Verneuil

Q5 Domrémy

Q6 Kingdom of England, Kingdom of France, and Duchy of Burgundy

Q7 Hail storm

Q8 1346

Q9 Reims Campaign

Q10 Richard II of England and Charles VI of France

Wars of the Roses 1 (easy)

Q1 Kingdom of England

Q2 Plantagenet

Q3 3

Q4 Battle of Bosworth Field

Q5 15th

Q6 Henry VI

Q7 White

Q8 Staffordshire

Q9 Edward IV

Q10 Henry VI

Wars of the Roses 2 (average)

Q1 House of York and House of Lancaster

Q2 Henry VII of England and Elizabeth of York

Q3 First Battle of St Albans

Q4 Duke of York

Q5 Edward V of England and Richard of Shrewsbury, Duke of York

Q6 Tower of London

Q7 Richard Neville, Earl of Warwick

Q8 *Game of Thrones*

Q9 Duke of Gloucester

Q10 3

Wars of the Roses 3 (expert)

Q1 Edmund, Earl of Rutland

Q2 Battle of Barnet

Q3 1470

Q4 1485

Q5 *Titulus Regius*

Q6 Lambert Simnel

Q7 The Princes in the Tower

Q8 Flemish

Q9 Uncle

Q10 1469

Thirty Years' War 1 (easy)

Q1 Europe

Q2 Frederick IV, Elector Palatine

Q3 Ferdinand II

Q4 Prague

Q5 Bohemia

Q6 Portugal

Q7 Witchcraft

Q8 A prison

Q9 Spain and Austria

Q10 1659

<u>Thirty Years' War 2 (average)</u>

Q1 Kingdom of Bohemia
Q2 The Peace of Westphalia
Q3 Catholicism and Protestantism
Q4 Lutheranism and Roman Catholicism
Q5 France
Q6 Sweden
Q7 France and Sweden
Q8 Brother-in-law
Q9 Spanish Empire
Q10 Bohemian Revolt

<u>Thirty Years' War 3 (expert)</u>

Q1 Osnabrück and Münster
Q2 1620
Q3 Officials being thrown out a window
Q4 The Winter King
Q5 1629
Q6 John George I, Elector of Saxony
Q7 Witch trials
Q8 The Bohemian Revolt, the Danish intervention, the Swedish intervention, and the French intervention
Q9 Huguenots
Q10 1629-31

<u>English Civil War 1 (easy)</u>

Q1 Roundheads
Q2 Charles I
Q3 Commonwealth of England
Q4 Oliver Cromwell
Q5 1660
Q6 Puritanism
Q7 1640
Q8 Execution

Q9 The New Model Army

Q10 Boscobel House

English Civil War 2 (average)

Q1 1649

Q2 Charles II of England

Q3 Wars of the Three Kingdoms

Q4 Thomas Fairfax

Q5 Battle of Naseby

Q6 3

Q7 Warwickshire

Q8 Oxford

Q9 Archbishop of Canterbury

Q10 Henrietta Maria of France

English Civil War 3 (expert)

Q1 Richard Cromwell

Q2 1648

Q3 The High Court of Justice

Q4 1649-60

Q5 The Ironsides

Q6 The Covenanters

Q7 Earl of Leven

Q8 The English Council of State

Q9 Sir John Hotham

Q10 The Grand Remonstrance

War of the Spanish Succession (average)

Q1 18th

Q2 Charles II of Spain

Q3 The Grand Alliance and the Bourbon Alliance

Q4 Kingdom of France and Holy Roman Empire

Q5 1713-15

Q6 Maria Theresa of Spain

Q7 Holy Roman Empire, Dutch Republic, and England

Q8 Kingdom of Hungary

Q9 Menorca and Gibraltar

Q10 France and the Dutch Republic

American Revolutionary War 1 (easy)

Q1 Yorktown

Q2 1780

Q3 George III

Q4 Province of Massachusetts Bay

Q5 Philadelphia

Q6 France

Q7 Atlantic Ocean

Q8 1775

Q9 Boston

Q10 George Washington

American Revolutionary War 2 (average)

Q1 Treaty of Paris

Q2 Horatio Gates

Q3 56

Q4 South Carolina

Q5 William Howe

Q6 The Bahamas

Q7 Thomas Paine

Q8 Spain and the Netherlands

Q9 The Battles of Lexington and Concord

Q10 Quebec City

American Revolutionary War 3 (expert)

Q1 The Conway Cabal

Q2 Expédition Particulière

Q3 François Joseph Paul de Grasse

Q4 Ninety Six

Q5 Vermont Republic

Q6 1778

Q7 Province of Georgia

Q8 Colony of Rhode Island and Providence Plantations

Q9 North Sea

Q10 Emanuel Leutze

French Revolution 1 (easy)

Q1 *La Marseillaise*

Q2 Austria

Q3 2 days

Q4 Maximilien Robespierre

Q5 Louis XVI of France

Q6 The *Ancien Régime*

Q7 Geneva

Q8 Thomas Jefferson

Q9 1791

Q10 Sweden

French Revolution 2 (average)

Q1 1793-94

Q2 French Revolutionary Wars

Q3 The Insurrection of 10 August 1792

Q4 1793

Q5 Commoners

Q6 Absolute monarchy

Q7 The Third Estate

Q8 Louis XVIII of France

Q9 Varennes

Q10 Political faction

French Revolution 3 (expert)

Q1 1789

Q2 The Committee of Public Safety

Q3 Bernard-René Jourdan de Launay

Q4 The French Republican calendar

Q5 Mirabeau

Q6 1790
Q7 The Mountain
Q8 Pillnitz Castle
Q9 Jean-Paul Marat
Q10 Jean-Paul Marat

Napoleonic Wars 1 (easy)

Q1 Battle of Austerlitz
Q2 1804
Q3 House of Bourbon
Q4 Alexander I
Q5 United Kingdom
Q6 1812
Q7 French Empire
Q8 Russia
Q9 Francis II, Holy Roman Emperor
Q10 Frankfurt proposals

Napoleonic Wars 2 (average)

Q1 1815
Q2 The Hundred Days
Q3 Peninsular War
Q4 1813-14
Q5 7
Q6 Joseph Bonaparte (his brother)
Q7 Congress of Vienna
Q8 The Coup of 18 Brumaire
Q9 United Kingdom
Q10 The Rosetta Stone

Napoleonic Wars 3 (expert)

Q1 Elba and Saint Helena
Q2 *Grande Armée*
Q3 Fyodor Rostopchin
Q4 Battle of Jena–Auerstedt

Q5 François-Paul Brueys d'Aigalliers
Q6 United Kingdom
Q7 Poland
Q8 John Moore
Q9 Spain
Q10 Switzerland

Crimean War (average)

Q1 1854-55
Q2 1853-56
Q3 British Empire and French Empire
Q4 Naval battle
Q5 1854
Q6 James Brudenell, Earl of Cardigan
Q7 Florence Nightingale
Q8 Treaty of Paris (1856)
Q9 Nicholas I and Alexander II
Q10 Photographer

American Civil War 1 (easy)

Q1 Fort Sumter
Q2 South Carolina
Q3 First Battle of Bull Run
Q4 Abraham Lincoln
Q5 11
Q6 Jefferson Davis
Q7 Mississippi
Q8 Reconstruction era
Q9 New Mexico Territory
Q10 Sand Creek massacre

American Civil War 2 (average)

Q1 Anaconda Plan
Q2 Shiloh
Q3 Ford's Theatre

Q4 Alfred Pleasonton
Q5 Daniel Decatur Emmett
Q6 Appomattox Court House
Q7 Charleston, South Carolina
Q8 Chicago, Illinois
Q9 Ironclad warships
Q10 Eastern Theatre

American Civil War 3 (expert)

Q1 Daniel Hough
Q2 Samuel J. Seymour
Q3 Missouri
Q4 Baltimore, Maryland
Q5 Henry Wirz
Q6 George B. McClellan
Q7 CSS *Virginia*
Q8 William Sherman
Q9 Army of Northern Virginia
Q10 John Singleton Mosby

Franco-Prussian War (average)

Q1 Alsace and Lorraine
Q2 French Third Republic
Q3 Germany
Q4 Napoleon III
Q5 Louis-Jules Trochu
Q6 Treaty of Frankfurt
Q7 Wilhelm I
Q8 1871
Q9 Otto von Bismarck
Q10 Chief of Staff

First World War 1 (easy)

Q1 Germany and Mexico
Q2 RMS *Lusitania*

Q3 Serbian

Q4 German

Q5 Russia

Q6 1917

Q7 Treaty of Versailles

Q8 The war to end all wars

Q9 3

Q10 North Sea

First World War 2 (average)

Q1 Germany, Austria-Hungary and Italy

Q2 Alfred von Schlieffen

Q3 House of Windsor

Q4 Field Marshall

Q5 Woodrow Wilson

Q6 Second Battle of Ypres

Q7 The Triple Entente

Q8 United Kingdom and France

Q9 Paul von Hindenburg

Q10 Royal Navy

First World War 3 (expert)

Q1 Italy

Q2 Dutch

Q3 John French

Q4 Treaty of London

Q5 Battle of Amiens

Q6 1916-17

Q7 The Grand Fleet and the High Seas Fleet

Q8 Blockade of Germany

Q9 Tank

Q10 Alexander Samsonov

<u>Russian Civil War (average)</u>

Q1 The Whites
Q2 Alexander Vasilyevich Kolchak
Q3 The Black Sea Fleet of the Imperial Russian Navy
Q4 Finland, Estonia, Latvia, Lithuania, and Poland
Q5 Cheka
Q6 1918
Q7 USA
Q8 Vladimir Lenin
Q9 The Bolsheviks
Q10 Samara

<u>Spanish Civil War (average)</u>

Q1 1936-39
Q2 Francisco Franco
Q3 1937
Q4 Nationalist faction and Republican faction
Q5 Manuel Azaña
Q6 Non-intervention
Q7 Italy and Germany
Q8 The Republicans showed a raised fist whereas the Nationalists gave the Roman salute
Q9 The White Terror
Q10 The Aragon Offensive

<u>Second World War 1 (easy)</u>

Q1 Jews
Q2 Joseph Goebbels
Q3 V-2
Q4 Austria
Q5 Nuremburg
Q6 Spitfire
Q7 Mediterranean and Middle East Theatre
Q8 Erwin Rommel

Q9 1933

Q10 Boeing B-29 Superfortress

Second World War 2 (average)

Q1 Doolittle Raid (also known as the Tokyo Raid)

Q2 Lightning War

Q3 Molotov–Ribbentrop Pact

Q4 Crimean

Q5 6th June 1944

Q6 Prague

Q7 The Philippines

Q8 Eva Braun

Q9 Air force

Q10 Battle of the River Plate

Second World War 3 (expert)

Q1 Germania

Q2 D-Day

Q3 Battle of Kursk

Q4 The Western Desert Campaign (Desert War)

Q5 The Battle of the Coral Sea

Q6 Battle of Midway

Q7 USS *Enterprise*

Q8 1906 election

Q9 George Marshall

Q10 Uncle Joe

Korean War (average)

Q1 Kim Il-sung

Q2 1953

Q3 President of South Korea

Q4 United Nations

Q5 38th parallel north

Q6 China and the Soviet Union

Q7 Japan

Q8 Hangang Bridge

Q9 Yellow Sea

Q10 X Corps

Vietnam War 1 (easy)

Q1 Aerial bombardment campaign

Q2 5

Q3 USS *Maddox*

Q4 Burning his draft card

Q5 Laos

Q6 Richard Nixon

Q7 Booby trap

Q8 Boat people

Q9 Hanoi

Q10 Bill Clinton

Vietnam War 2 (average)

Q1 Robert McNamara

Q2 1968

Q3 United States Congress

Q4 Agent Orange

Q5 Ho Chi Minh trail

Q6 National Liberation Front

Q7 Domino theory

Q8 Fall of Saigon

Q9 Ho Chi Minh City

Q10 John McCain

Vietnam War 3 (expert)

Q1 1968

Q2 The Hanoi Hilton

Q3 1972

Q4 Operation Apache Snow

Q5 Police action

Q6 Bell UH-1 Iroquois

Q7 1973

Q8 Nick Ut (also known as Huỳnh Công Út)

Q9 Kent State University

Q10 Oliver Stone

Answers: Ancient World

Ancient Egypt 1 (easy)

Q1 Life
Q2 Cobra
Q3 Luxor
Q4 British Museum
Q5 Howard Carter
Q6 Ramesses II
Q7 Ra
Q8 Menes
Q9 31st century BC
Q10 Second Intermediate Period

Ancient Egypt 2 (average)

Q1 Upper and Lower Egypt
Q2 Thutmose I
Q3 Hittites
Q4 The realm of the dead
Q5 Ptolemy V
Q6 Ay
Q7 Lower Egypt
Q8 London, Paris and New York
Q9 Pyramid of Djoser
Q10 East bank

Ancient Egypt 3 (expert)

Q1 Ineni
Q2 Stomach, intestines, lungs and liver
Q3 Nebkheperura
Q4 Flinders Petrie
Q5 KV62
Q6 Flinders Petrie
Q7 Manetho
Q8 The Pyramid Texts

Q9 Sahure

Q10 Achaemenid Empire

<u>Ancient Greece 1 (easy)</u>

Q1 Macedonia

Q2 Athens

Q3 Healing temple

Q4 Mausoleum

Q5 Cecrops I

Q6 Roman Republic

Q7 Sculptor

Q8 Italy

Q9 Bronze

Q10 Athens

<u>Ancient Greece 2 (average)</u>

Q1 Linear B script

Q2 Troy

Q3 *Kotinos* (olive wreath)

Q4 To fight the Persian Empire following the Greek victory at the Battle of Plataea

Q5 Plato

Q6 Athenian democracy

Q7 Crete

Q8 Sparta

Q9 The major deities of the Greek pantheon

Q10 Male

<u>Ancient Greece 3 (expert)</u>

Q1 Arthur Evans

Q2 Delphi

Q3 Delian League (Athens) and Peloponnesian League (Sparta)

Q4 Battle of Heraclea and Battle of Asculum

Q5 Mathematician

Q6 Mycenaean Greece

Q7 Chalcis and Eretria

Q8 Pythia

Q9 Philip II of Macedon

Q10 An analogue computer

Ancient Rome 1 (easy)

Q1 Augustus

Q2 Sesterce

Q3 Constantine

Q4 Rubicon

Q5 Visigoths

Q6 Shield

Q7 Julius Caesar

Q8 3

Q9 7

Q10 Chariot racing

Ancient Rome 2 (average)

Q1 Romulus and Remus

Q2 Syria

Q3 Herculaneum

Q4 Emperor Claudius

Q5 Vespasian

Q6 Trajan

Q7 Battle of Actium

Q8 Spartacus

Q9 Stoicism

Q10 SPQR

Ancient Rome 3 (expert)

Q1 Trier

Q2 Bath

Q3 Eruption of Mount Vesuvius 79AD

Q4 The Roman Kingdom, the Roman Republic, and the Roman Empire

Q5 Nerva, Trajan, Hadrian, Antoninus Pius, and Marcus Aurelius

Q6 Ravenna

Q7 The Senones
Q8 Pitched battles
Q9 Ancient Greek culture
Q10 Licinius, Emperor of the Roman Empire

Answers: Pre-Columbian Americas

<u>North America 1 (easy)</u>

Q1 St Louis, Missouri
Q2 United Kingdom
Q3 Bering Strait
Q4 Virginia
Q5 Buffalo
Q6 Archaeological site
Q7 Mississippi River
Q8 Florida
Q9 Great Plains
Q10 Alberta

<u>North America 2 (average)</u>

Q1 Sacagawea
Q2 Archaic period
Q3 Paleo-Indians
Q4 Oklahoma
Q5 Mounds
Q6 Monks Mound
Q7 France
Q8 A person of mixed Native American and European ancestry
Q9 Battle of the Thames
Q10 Scalp

<u>North America 3 (expert)</u>

Q1 Miami people
Q2 Woodland period
Q3 Mississippian culture
Q4 Cherokee, Chickasaw, Choctaw, Creek (Muskogee), and Seminole
Q5 Arawak
Q6 Clovis culture
Q7 British Columbia
Q8 *Skræling*

Q9 Eaters of raw meat

Q10 Yosemite Valley

<u>Maya 1 (easy)</u>

Q1 Codices

Q2 Chichen Itza

Q3 3rd century BC

Q4 Stone

Q5 Blue

Q6 Paper

Q7 1697

Q8 Sun

Q9 Pyramid

Q10 Underworld

<u>Maya 2 (average)</u>

Q1 Kukulkan

Q2 Guatemala

Q3 Tikal

Q4 Patrilineal

Q5 Preclassic period

Q6 Tula

Q7 Obsidian

Q8 Honduras

Q9 Food

Q10 Currency

<u>Maya 3 (expert)</u>

Q1 20

Q2 The Peten Itza kingdom

Q3 Ulama

Q4 Cyrus Longworth Lundell

Q5 K'inich Janaab' Pakal

Q6 *Dresden Codex*, *Madrid Codex*, and *Paris Codex*

Q7 Hunahpu and Xbalanque

Q8 K'iche' people
Q9 Crossed eyes
Q10 Postclassic period

<u>Aztec 1 (easy)</u>

Q1 Mexico City
Q2 Fifth
Q3 Acamapichtli
Q4 City state
Q5 Flower Wars
Q6 *Tlacochcalcatl*
Q7 Long-distance merchants
Q8 Sumptuary laws
Q9 Nezahualcoyotl
Q10 Templo Mayor

<u>Aztec 2 (average)</u>

Q1 Triple Alliance
Q2 Mexico City Cathedral
Q3 Bernardino de Sahagún
Q4 Azcapotzalco
Q5 Tlatelolco
Q6 Smallpox
Q7 Tarascan state
Q8 Tlaloc
Q9 7
Q10 Prickly pear cactus

<u>Aztec 3 (expert)</u>

Q1 *Chinampas*
Q2 Tlatelolco
Q3 Tezcatlipoca
Q4 Cuauhtémoc
Q5 A strategy game
Q6 Aztlán

Q7 Smoking shield

Q8 Skull rack

Q9 *Calpulli*

Q10 Slaves

Inca 1 (easy)

Q1 Inti

Q2 Atahualpa

Q3 Cuzco

Q4 Francisco Pizarro

Q5 4

Q6 Language family

Q7 15th century

Q8 1531

Q9 3

Q10 Children

Inca 2 (average)

Q1 Urubamba Valley

Q2 Hiram Bingham III

Q3 Province/region

Q4 Huayna Capac

Q5 High Priests of the Sun

Q6 Inti Raymi

Q7 Nazca Lines

Q8 A citadel

Q9 Cajamarca

Q10 Neo-Inca State

Inca 3 (expert)

Q1 A ritual stone, associated with the astronomic clock or calendar of the Inca

Q2 *Huaca*

Q3 Pachamama

Q4 Wari Empire and Tiwanaku Empire

Q5 Huáscar and Atahualpa

Q6 Compulsory public service (tribute in the form of labour)
Q7 Battle of the Maule
Q8 Drinking vessel
Q9 1572
Q10 Vilcabamba

Answers: English Monarchs

William I (easy)

Q1 The Bastard
Q2 2
Q3 Battle of Hastings
Q4 Rouen
Q5 French
Q6 3 months
Q7 Built castles
Q8 Church of England
Q9 Westminster Abbey
Q10 Robert Curthose

William I (average)

Q1 December 25th (Christmas Day)
Q2 Matilda of Flanders
Q3 Robert Curthose
Q4 Guy of Burgundy
Q5 1086
Q6 Battle Abbey
Q7 2
Q8 Lanfranc
Q9 New Forest
Q10 Riding a horse

William I (expert)

Q1 First cousin once removed
Q2 Herluin de Conteville
Q3 Pevensey Bay
Q4 1069-70
Q5 Isle of Ely, East Anglia
Q6 Treaty of Abernethy
Q7 1035
Q8 19

Q9 Earl of Kent and Bishop of Bayeux
Q10 Nearly 70 m

Willliam II (average)

Q1 New Forest
Q2 *Rufus* is Latin for 'the Red' and he had red hair
Q3 0
Q4 The spot where William II fell after being struck by an arrow
Q5 Odo of Bayeux
Q6 Anselm
Q7 Malcom III of Scotland
Q8 First Crusade
Q9 *Anglo-Saxon Chronicle*
Q10 Winchester Cathedral

Henry I (easy)

Q1 The *White Ship*
Q2 2
Q3 The Anarchy
Q4 3
Q5 Normandy
Q6 Edward the Confessor
Q7 The Coronation Charter
Q8 Normandy
Q9 1135
Q10 Imprisoned

Henry I (average)

Q1 Duchy of Normandy
Q2 His brother (Robert Curthose)
Q3 To produce a male heir
Q4 2
Q5 He was returning from the First Crusade
Q6 Matilda
Q7 Anselm

Q8 Henry V, Holy Roman Emperor

Q9 Louis VI of France

Q10 Lampreys

Henry I (expert)

Q1 Reading Abbey

Q2 Maurice, the Bishop of London

Q3 1101

Q4 1106

Q5 Exotic animals

Q6 1130

Q7 Thomas FitzStephen

Q8 Fulk V, Count of Anjou

Q9 Bishop of Winchester

Q10 Philip I and Louis VI

Stephen and Matilda (easy)

Q1 The Anarchy

Q2 Uncle

Q3 Plantagenet

Q4 King Stephen

Q5 0

Q6 Second Crusade

Q7 Edith

Q8 Rouen Cathedral

Q9 1125

Q10 Peace

Stephen and Matilda (average)

Q1 Stephen of Blois

Q2 Eustace IV, Count of Boulogne

Q3 Matilda's son (Henry II)

Q4 William Adelin

Q5 Deeds of King Stephen (or Acts of Stephen)

Q6 Henry II

Q7 King Stephen
Q8 Flanders
Q9 Lady of the English
Q10 Gloucester

<u>Stephen and Matilda (expert)</u>

Q1 1135-53
Q2 His wife (Queen Matilda of Boulogne)
Q3 Oxford Castle
Q4 Faversham Abbey
Q5 Blois
Q6 St. Peter's Basilica
Q7 William de Corbeil
Q8 3
Q9 Battle of Ramla
Q10 William I, Count of Boulogne

<u>Henry II (easy)</u>

Q1 3
Q2 Thomas Becket
Q3 Plantagenet
Q4 Kingdom of France
Q5 Red
Q6 French and Latin
Q7 Winchester Cathedral
Q8 Ireland
Q9 Imprisoned
Q10 Jerusalem

<u>Henry II (average)</u>

Q1 Eleanor of Aquitaine
Q2 John
Q3 Treaty of Wallingford
Q4 Curtmantle
Q5 Louis VII of France

Q6 Angevin Empire
Q7 Perforated ulcer
Q8 High King of Ireland
Q9 Pope Alexander III
Q10 Count of Anjou

<u>Henry II (expert)</u>

Q1 Château de Chinon
Q2 1170-83
Q3 4
Q4 First (and only) English pope
Q5 1164
Q6 Edward Grim
Q7 William I (the Lion) of Scotland
Q8 Eleanor of Aquitaine (wife), Henry the Young King (son), Richard I (son), and Geoffrey II, Duke of Brittany (son)
Q9 English law
Q10 Fontevraud Abbey

<u>Richard I (easy)</u>

Q1 6 months
Q2 The Lionheart
Q3 Third
Q4 His mother
Q5 Acre
Q6 1189
Q7 Kingdom of Jerusalem
Q8 York
Q9 Saladin
Q10 The Pope

<u>Richard I (average)</u>

Q1 Aquitaine
Q2 Berengaria of Navarre
Q3 Philip II of France

Q4 Saladin

Q5 Chancellor of England

Q6 Their father (Henry II of England)

Q7 Jews

Q8 Sicily

Q9 Rouen

Q10 Crossbow

Richard I (expert)

Q1 Fontevraud Abbey

Q2 Burgruine Dürnstein

Q3 Hodierna of St Albans

Q4 Third Crusade

Q5 Anti-Semitic riots

Q6 The capture of Jerusalem by Saladin

Q7 High Sheriff of Nottinghamshire, Derbyshire and the Royal Forests

Q8 Arthur I, Duke of Brittany

Q9 Cyprus

Q10 Limassol

John (easy)

Q1 Great Charter

Q2 Lackland

Q3 Henry II

Q4 Innocent III

Q5 2

Q6 Dysentery

Q7 William the Lion

Q8 Runneymede

Q9 Stephen Langton

Q10 The First Barons' War

John (average)

Q1 Worcester

Q2 Angevin Empire

Q3 Ireland

Q4 Philip II of France

Q5 Robin Hood

Q6 His father (Henry II)

Q7 Arthur I, Duke of Brittany

Q8 Archbishop of Canterbury

Q9 Louis VIII of France

Q10 The Crown Jewels

John (expert)

Q1 Anglo-French War (1213–1214)

Q2 Isabella, Countess of Gloucester

Q3 Buy his loyalty while Richard I was away on crusade

Q4 He was the son of Henry II's eldest son, Geoffrey II, Duke of Brittany

Q5 5

Q6 1202-04

Q7 Marcher Lord

Q8 Henry II, Henry the Young King, Richard I, John, and Henry III

Q9 Llywelyn the Great

Q10 Welsh uprising of 1211

Henry III (average)

Q1 Henry of Winchester

Q2 First Barons' War

Q3 Kingdom of France

Q4 Eleanor of Provence

Q5 Earl of Leicester

Q6 Edward the Confessor

Q7 Jews

Q8 1259

Q9 Simon de Montfort

Q10 University of Northampton

Edward I (average)

Q1 Eleanor of Castile, Queen of England
Q2 Edward Longshanks and the Hammer of the Scots
Q3 Jews
Q4 Wales
Q5 Scotland and France
Q6 Ninth Crusade
Q7 Prince of Wales
Q8 Castles
Q9 First War of Scottish Independence
Q10 Smithfield

Edward II (average)

Q1 Hot poker inserted up the anus
Q2 Piers Gaveston
Q3 Robert the Bruce
Q4 Roger Mortimer
Q5 Hugh Despenser the Younger and Hugh Despenser the Elder
Q6 1322
Q7 Gloucester Cathedral
Q8 His son (Edward III)
Q9 Ordinances of 1311
Q10 Pontefract Castle

Edward III (average)

Q1 The Hundred Years' War
Q2 Nottingham Castle
Q3 Mistress
Q4 The Black Death
Q5 French
Q6 Edward of Woodstock (the Black Prince)
Q7 Philippa of Hainault
Q8 Battle of Crécy (1346) and Battle of Poitiers (1356)
Q9 Naval
Q10 John II of France

Richard II (easy)

Q1 White Hart
Q2 Westminster Abbey
Q3 Under a year
Q4 Edward III
Q5 14
Q6 Pontefract Castle
Q7 The Western Schism
Q8 Scotland
Q9 Wife
Q10 The Tyranny

Richard II (average)

Q1 2
Q2 Edward of Woodstock (The Black Prince)
Q3 Wat Tyler
Q4 Westminster Hall
Q5 Geoffrey Chaucer
Q6 Poll tax
Q7 Simon Sudbury
Q8 Hundred Years' War
Q9 Calais
Q10 Thomas of Woodstock, Duke of Gloucester; Richard FitzAlan, Earl of Arundel and of Surrey; and Thomas de Beauchamp, Earl of Warwick

Richard II (expert)

Q1 Kent
Q2 Savoy Palace
Q3 Chronicling the reign of Richard II
Q4 1386
Q5 William Walworth
Q6 1388
Q7 Bordeaux, Duchy of Aquitaine
Q8 10

Q9 1394
Q10 Charles VI of France

Henry IV (average)

Q1 Henry Bolingbroke
Q2 Nephew
Q3 Richard II
Q4 House of Lancaster
Q5 John of Gaunt
Q6 2
Q7 1399-1400
Q8 Lords Appellant
Q9 Henry Percy
Q10 Canterbury Cathedral

Henry V (average)

Q1 Henry of Monmouth
Q2 1415
Q3 Henry V and his heirs would inherit the Kingdom of France after the death of Charles VI of France
Q4 Surgeon
Q5 Lollard
Q6 Holy Roman Empire
Q7 1415
Q8 Dysentery
Q9 1
Q10 Edmund Mortimer, Earl of March

Henry VI (easy)

Q1 Kingdom of France
Q2 1
Q3 Catholic
Q4 Burned at the stake
Q5 The Wars of the Roses
Q6 Lancaster

Q7 3
Q8 Madness
Q9 English Channel
Q10 St Paul's Cathedral

Henry VI (average)

Q1 Margaret of Anjou
Q2 Tower of London
Q3 2
Q4 Notre-Dame de Paris
Q5 Edward of Westminster, Prince of Wales
Q6 Second Battle of St Albans
Q7 Windsor Castle
Q8 Louis XI of France
Q9 9 months
Q10 Hundred Years' War

Henry VI (expert)

Q1 Eton College; King's College, Cambridge; and All Souls College, Oxford
Q2 The Maid of Orléans
Q3 John of Lancaster, Duke of Bedford
Q4 1435
Q5 Duke of Suffolk
Q6 1450
Q7 The restoration of Henry VI in 1470
Q8 Her parents
Q9 Battle of Northampton
Q10 Maternal grandfather

Edward IV (average)

Q1 Edmund, Earl of Rutland
Q2 Elizabeth Woodville
Q3 2
Q4 House of York
Q5 George, Duke of Clarence

Q6 Edward of Westminster, Prince of Wales
Q7 1470
Q8 Richard Neville, Earl of Warwick
Q9 Herefordshire
Q10 Rouen

Edward V (average)

Q1 Richard of Shrewsbury, Duke of York
Q2 1483
Q3 Lord Protector
Q4 Ludlow
Q5 Titulus Regius
Q6 Tower of London
Q7 Westminster Abbey
Q8 Anthony Woodville, 2nd Earl Rivers (his uncle)
Q9 John Argentine
Q10 Thomas More

Richard III (easy)

Q1 Henry VII
Q2 Gloucester
Q3 York
Q4 Leicester Cathedral
Q5 Nephews
Q6 Thomas More
Q7 Yorkshire
Q8 Catholic
Q9 1483
Q10 Richard III

Richard III (average)

Q1 1485
Q2 White boar
Q3 Edward of Middleham
Q4 Richard Neville, Earl of Warwick (The Kingmaker)

Q5 Henry Stafford, Duke of Buckingham

Q6 Edward V

Q7 Wars of the Roses

Q8 1

Q9 Thomas Bourchier

Q10 1484

Richard III (expert)

Q1 University of Leicester

Q2 Northampton

Q3 *Titulus Regius*

Q4 William Hastings

Q5 Robert Stillington, Bishop of Bath and Wells

Q6 Thomas Stanley

Q7 Francis Lovell, William Catesby and William Ratcliffe

Q8 Idiopathic scoliosis

Q9 Lord Protector of England

Q10 Henry Percy, Earl of Northumberland

Henry VII (average)

Q1 Margaret Beaufort

Q2 Richard III

Q3 Pembroke Castle

Q4 Tudor

Q5 Wales

Q6 Lambert Simnel

Q7 Belgium

Q8 Arthur, Prince of Wales

Q9 Elizabeth of York

Q10 Uncle

Henry VIII (easy)

Q1 6

Q2 Protestantism

Q3 Faith

Q4 3
Q5 Monasteries
Q6 Kingdom of France
Q7 16
Q8 Charles I of England
Q9 Kingdom of Scotland
Q10 Ship

Henry VIII (average)

Q1 Jane Seymour
Q2 Anne Boleyn and Catherine Howard
Q3 Supreme Head of the Church of England
Q4 Thomas More
Q5 King of Ireland
Q6 Ferdinand II of Aragon and Isabella I of Castile
Q7 Pope Clement VII
Q8 Palace of Whitehall
Q9 Beheading
Q10 1509

Henry VIII (expert)

Q1 Laws in Wales Acts 1535 and 1542
Q2 1546
Q3 Catherine of Aragon
Q4 Henry, Duke of Cornwall
Q5 Non-aggression pact
Q6 The *Defence of the Seven Sacraments*
Q7 Anne Boleyn
Q8 Isle of White
Q9 Refuse the Oath of Supremacy
Q10 Richard Foxe

Edward VI (average)

Q1 Jane Seymour
Q2 Protestantism

Q3 Barnaby Fitzpatrick

Q4 *The Prince and the Pauper*

Q5 First cousin once removed

Q6 Edward Seymour, Duke of Somerset

Q7 15

Q8 Kingdom of Scotland

Q9 Hampton Court Palace

Q10 16

Mary I (average)

Q1 Roman Catholicism

Q2 Philip II of Spain

Q3 Catherine of Aragon

Q4 Bloody Mary

Q5 Lady Jane Grey

Q6 0

Q7 John Dudley, Duke of Northumberland

Q8 Wyatt's Rebellion

Q9 Thomas Cranmer

Q10 1558

Elizabeth I (easy)

Q1 Tudor

Q2 Anne Boleyn

Q3 Protestantism

Q4 Anglo-Spanish War

Q5 130

Q6 0

Q7 Privateer

Q8 Kingdom of Scotland

Q9 Kingdom of Spain

Q10 Leicester

<u>Elizabeth I (average)</u>

Q1 Mirrors
Q2 The Virgin Queen, Gloriana or Good Queen Bess
Q3 William Cecil
Q4 Mary, Queen of Scots
Q5 1588
Q6 William Shakespeare
Q7 *Golden Hind*
Q8 Christopher Marlowe
Q9 Francis, Duke of Anjou
Q10 Richmond Palace

<u>Elizabeth I (expert)</u>

Q1 Act of Supremacy 1534
Q2 Alonso Pérez de Guzmán, Duke of Medina Sidonia
Q3 Playwright
Q4 Margaret Bryan
Q5 Kat
Q6 The Succession to the Crown Act
Q7 25
Q8 Owen Oglethorpe, Catholic Bishop of Carlisle
Q9 First cousins once removed
Q10 Abd el-Ouahed ben Messaoud

<u>James I (easy)</u>

Q1 Robert Catesby
Q2 Scotland
Q3 Stuart
Q4 1611
Q5 1603
Q6 1
Q7 Anne of Denmark
Q8 Murder
Q9 Edinburgh Castle
Q10 State

James I (average)

Q1 Mary, Queen of Scots
Q2 Jacobean era
Q3 Combine them
Q4 The Americas
Q5 5th November
Q6 Henry Frederick, Prince of Wales
Q7 George Villiers
Q8 1618
Q9 Hung, drawn and quartered
Q10 Thirty Years' War

James I (expert)

Q1 Henry VI of England
Q2 *Daemonologie*
Q3 James Stewart, Earl of Moray
Q4 Lady Arbella Stuart
Q5 Isle of Lewis
Q6 1614
Q7 Architect
Q8 1613
Q9 Puritans
Q10 Plantation of Ulster

Charles I (easy)

Q1 The English Civil War
Q2 Scotland
Q3 2
Q4 1649
Q5 Oliver Cromwell
Q6 Thomas Fairfax
Q7 Carisbrooke Castle
Q8 England, Scotland and Ireland
Q9 The English Parliament
Q10 Beheaded

Charles I (average)

Q1 Henrietta Maria of France
Q2 Parliament
Q3 Commonwealth of England
Q4 Palace of Whitehall
Q5 The New Model Army
Q6 The Personal Rule (or the Eleven Years' Tyranny)
Q7 High treason
Q8 North Yorkshire
Q9 Prince Rupert of the Rhine
Q10 Henry Stuart, Duke of Gloucester

Charles I (expert)

Q1 Commission of array
Q2 The divine right of kings
Q3 William Laud
Q4 The Greyhound
Q5 John Hampden, Arthur Haselrig, Denzil Holles, John Pym, and William Strode
Q6 3
Q7 Scottish Covenanters
Q8 Anthony van Dyck
Q9 Battle of Chalgrove Field
Q10 The Rump Parliament

Charles II (average)

Q1 Titus Oates
Q2 The Interregnum
Q3 1660
Q4 Oliver Cromwell
Q5 Mistress
Q6 18
Q7 Assassinate King Charles II of England and his brother (the future James II)
Q8 Monarch
Q9 0
Q10 Battle of Edgehill

James II (average)

Q1 The Glorious Revolution of 1688
Q2 Catholic
Q3 James Francis Edward Stuart
Q4 1
Q5 Jacobite
Q6 France
Q7 William III of England
Q8 Louis XIV of France
Q9 Declaration of Indulgence
Q10 Brother

William III and Mary II (average)

Q1 William of Orange
Q2 Dutch Republic
Q3 James II of England
Q4 Protestantism
Q5 William III
Q6 Kensington Palace
Q7 1689
Q8 The Immortal Seven
Q9 Bishop of London
Q10 Henry Purcell

Anne (easy)

Q1 Great Britain
Q2 Westminster Abbey
Q3 Church of England
Q4 Stuart
Q5 Prince William, Duke of Gloucester
Q6 1702
Q7 Whig
Q8 War of the Spanish Succession
Q9 Jacobites
Q10 1684

Anne (average)

Q1 St James's Palace
Q2 Tory
Q3 1706 and 1707
Q4 Sisters
Q5 Denmark
Q6 Palace of Whitehall
Q7 Lord High Admiral
Q8 1703
Q9 The royal touch
Q10 Second cousins

Anne (expert)

Q1 Duchess of Marlborough
Q2 James II of England
Q3 Eyes
Q4 11
Q5 17
Q6 Speaker of the House of Commons
Q7 Whig Junto
Q8 Lord President of the Council
Q9 Thomas Tenison
Q10 1683

George I (easy)

Q1 Elector of Hanover
Q2 Robert Walpole
Q3 1
Q4 Scotland
Q5 He was German
Q6 James I
Q7 6
Q8 Spain
Q9 Cousin
Q10 James Francis Edward Stuart

<u>George I (average)</u>

Q1 Whig
Q2 Hanover
Q3 Great Turkish War
Q4 Mistress
Q5 Rioting
Q6 Ahlden House
Q7 In Hanover he was an absolute ruler; in Britain he had to rule through Parliament
Q8 Act of Settlement
Q9 A stroke
Q10 Lutheranism

<u>George I (expert)</u>

Q1 Osnabrück
Q2 54
Q3 Philip Christoph von Königsmarck
Q4 Triple Alliance
Q5 Chapel of the Leineschloss
Q6 Earl of Mar
Q7 7
Q8 His son, the future George II
Q9 Ernest Augustus
Q10 Louis

<u>George II (easy)</u>

Q1 Grandson
Q2 Adultery
Q3 43
Q4 The War of Austrian Succession
Q5 Westminster Abbey
Q6 British Museum
Q7 *Pirates of the Caribbean*
Q8 1
Q9 George Augustus
Q10 Prince-elector

<u>George II (average)</u>

Q1 Outside Britain
Q2 1745
Q3 French
Q4 His father (George I)
Q5 Frederick, Prince of Wales
Q6 Betty Burke
Q7 1756
Q8 He'd lived longer than any of his British or English predecessors
Q9 University of Göttingen
Q10 The sides of his and his wife's coffins to be removed so their remains could mingle

<u>George II (expert)</u>

Q1 Battle of Dettingen
Q2 Kensington Palace
Q3 Sophia Naturalization Act
Q4 George Frideric Handel
Q5 A string of notable British victories over French-led opponents during the Seven Years' War (The term is taken from Latin, and is used to denote a 'year of miracles' or 'year of wonders').
Q6 1759
Q7 Aortic dissection
Q8 Trinity College, Dublin
Q9 Golden Square
Q10 359 Georgia

<u>George III (easy)</u>

Q1 1801
Q2 King of Hanover
Q3 English
Q4 North America
Q5 15
Q6 Earl of Chatham
Q7 Boston Tea Party

Q8 Anti-Catholic
Q9 2
Q10 James Hadfield

George III (average)

Q1 0
Q2 Napoleon Bonaparte
Q3 Mental illness
Q4 His son, Prince George (the future George IV)
Q5 His father's (Frederick, Prince of Wales)
Q6 Enlightenment
Q7 John Stuart, 3rd Earl of Bute
Q8 The North American colonies
Q9 Thirteen Colonies
Q10 John Adams

George III (expert)

Q1 Norfolk House
Q2 *Cato, a Tragedy*
Q3 Duchy of Mecklenburg-Strelitz
Q4 John Stuart, 3rd Earl of Bute
Q5 John Wilkes
Q6 Lord North
Q7 Perth Agreement
Q8 The King of Prussia
Q9 Francis Willis
Q10 William Grenville

George IV (average)

Q1 The Royal Pavilion
Q2 10
Q3 Caroline of Brunswick
Q4 Brothers
Q5 Dissolve his marriage
Q6 1

Q7 St George's Chapel
Q8 Thomas Secker
Q9 Ireland
Q10 Tory

William IV (average)

Q1 Buckingham Palace
Q2 The 'Sailor King'
Q3 10
Q4 The Slavery Abolition Act 1833
Q5 Niece
Q6 Midshipman
Q7 To enable him to pay off substantial debts
Q8 Belgium
Q9 His brother (Prince Adolphus, Duke of Cambridge)
Q10 The electoral system

Victoria (easy)

Q1 Hanover
Q2 Husband
Q3 10
Q4 Europe
Q5 8
Q6 Great Famine
Q7 Corn Laws
Q8 4
Q9 Scotland
Q10 Crimean War

Victoria (average)

Q1 Empress of India
Q2 Isle of White
Q3 Albert of Saxe-Coburg and Gotha
Q4 Fifth
Q5 William Lamb, 2nd Viscount Melbourne

Q6 Lady Flora Hastings

Q7 Louise Lehzen

Q8 Haemophilia

Q9 Benjamin Disraeli

Q10 East India Company

Victoria (expert)

Q1 18

Q2 9

Q3 Kensington System

Q4 Dash

Q5 Ernest Augustus

Q6 400,000

Q7 Edward Oxford

Q8 1838

Q9 Felice Orsini

Q10 Because of a curt reply from the queen in response to some poetry he'd mailed her

Edward VII (average)

Q1 The Home Fleet

Q2 Second Boer War

Q3 Edwardian

Q4 Kaiser Wilhelm II of Germany

Q5 Parliament Act 1911

Q6 Liberal

Q7 Denmark

Q8 Buckingham Palace (born and died)

Q9 House of Saxe-Coburg and Gotha

Q10 Diagnosed with appendicitis

George V (average)

Q1 Charlotte Bill

Q2 House of Commons

Q3 HMS *Britannia*

Q4 House of Windsor
Q5 Mary of Teck
Q6 Balfour Declaration
Q7 1924
Q8 Tsar Nicholas II of Russia
Q9 1932
Q10 Charles Sims

Edward VIII (average)

Q1 1936
Q2 Sixteenth
Q3 Wallis Simpson
Q4 France
Q5 Duke of Windsor
Q6 Adolf Hitler
Q7 Serve on the front line
Q8 Kidnap Edward VIII
Q9 Windsor
Q10 Marguerite Alibert

George VI (average)

Q1 Second World War
Q2 First Head of the Commonwealth and the last Emperor of India
Q3 Albert
Q4 The Queen Mother
Q5 Speech therapy
Q6 Louis Greig
Q7 Prince George, Duke of Kent
Q8 Edward Wood, 1st Earl of Halifax
Q9 United Nations
Q10 Colin Firth

Elizabeth II (average)

Q1 Auxiliary Territorial Service
Q2 16

Q3 Sapphire Jubilee

Q4 Diana, Princess of Wales

Q5 Winston Churchill

Q6 Prince Philip, Duke of Edinburgh

Q7 Princess Margaret, Countess of Snowdon

Q8 Geoffrey Fisher

Q9 Supreme Governor

Q10 Grenada

Answers: National and Regional Histories

Africa 1 (easy)

Q1 First World War
Q2 Mali Empire
Q3 Dutch
Q4 Zulu Kingdom
Q5 Ethiopia
Q6 1960
Q7 7th century AD
Q8 Algeria
Q9 Radama I
Q10 Madagascar

Africa 2 (average)

Q1 The Royal Palace of Oba of Benin
Q2 Henry Morton Stanley
Q3 The Gold Coast
Q4 Ashanti people
Q5 France
Q6 England
Q7 Ancient Egypt
Q8 Carthage
Q9 Juvénal Habyarimana
Q10 Kingdom of Zimbabwe

Africa 3 (expert)

Q1 Kumasi
Q2 Paul Kruger
Q3 1948
Q4 Julius Nyerere
Q5 Makuria
Q6 Khafra
Q7 Kingdom of Kongo
Q8 Gondar

Q9 Battle of Mbwila
Q10 Zambia

<u>Australia 1 (easy)</u>

Q1 60,000 years
Q2 Edmund Barton
Q3 6
Q4 Rum Rebellion
Q5 Cricket
Q6 Donkey
Q7 Aboriginal Australians
Q8 Didgeridoo
Q9 The Mutiny on the Bounty
Q10 1788

<u>Australia 2 (average)</u>

Q1 Matthew Flinders
Q2 1901
Q3 New South Wales
Q4 Anzac Day
Q5 Gallipoli Campaign
Q6 Harold Holt
Q7 House of Representatives and Senate
Q8 Thomas Townshend, Viscount Sydney
Q9 Tasmania
Q10 3

<u>Australia 3 (expert)</u>

Q1 Protectionist Party
Q2 The First Fleet
Q3 Gold miners
Q4 Nobody's land
Q5 26th January
Q6 Bidjigal
Q7 Joseph Banks

Q8 Port Jackson
Q9 Tahiti
Q10 1932-34

China 1 (easy)

Q1 Qin Shi Huang
Q2 Bamboo slips
Q3 Taiwan
Q4 Tiananmen Square
Q5 6
Q6 Republic of China
Q7 20th
Q8 Taiwan
Q9 The rule of the Emperor of China
Q10 Shaanxi

China 2 (average)

Q1 Square
Q2 Spring and Autumn period
Q3 Ming
Q4 Qing
Q5 1997
Q6 The Great Leap Forward
Q7 Puyi
Q8 Han Chinese
Q9 Hong Xiuquan
Q10 Manchuria

China 3 (expert)

Q1 Azure Dragon, Vermilion Bird, White Tiger and Black Turtle
Q2 Painter
Q3 Emperor Hung-wu
Q4 Manchu
Q5 61
Q6 Queues

Q7 1850-64
Q8 Li Hung-chang
Q9 Eastern Qing tombs
Q10 Sima Qian

India 1 (easy)

Q1 Hinduism
Q2 Mahatma Gandhi
Q3 Ustad Ahmad Lahori
Q4 Minaret
Q5 Ramananda
Q6 Fatehpur Sikri
Q7 1930
Q8 Kolkata
Q9 The Netherlands
Q10 19th and 20th

India 2 (average)

Q1 Buddhism
Q2 Rajendra Prased
Q3 1510
Q4 Indian National Congress
Q5 Samudragupta
Q6 Nanda
Q7 *Anandamath*
Q8 Arya Samaj
Q9 Harihara I
Q10 Indian Rebellion of 1857

India 3 (expert)

Q1 Warren Hastings
Q2 Akbar I (Mughal Empire) and Hemu (Sur Empire)
Q3 Birbal
Q4 Lord Dalhousie (Governor-General of India)
Q5 Sikandar Lodi

Q6 Aurangzeb
Q7 Panini
Q8 Buddhist, Hindu and Jain
Q9 The Pratihara Empire, the Pala Empire and the Rashtrakuta Empire
Q10 3rd century BC

Japan 1 (easy)

Q1 7th century BC
Q2 Shinto
Q3 Portugal
Q4 World War Two
Q5 At sea
Q6 William II
Q7 Dress
Q8 Stringed
Q9 Kyoto
Q10 Meiji period

Japan 2 (average)

Q1 Hari-kari
Q2 Edo
Q3 Shōgun
Q4 National Foundation Day
Q5 16th and 19th centuries
Q6 Isolationist
Q7 16th century
Q8 Northern Court
Q9 William Adams
Q10 Wa

Japan 3 (expert)

Q1 Jōmon period
Q2 Taira and Minamoto clans
Q3 Heian period
Q4 1853

Q5 *Kojiki*
Q6 Nakatomi clan
Q7 Portugal
Q8 Asuka period
Q9 Architect
Q10 Edo period

Russia 1 (easy)

Q1 Peter the Great
Q2 Alexander II
Q3 2
Q4 St Petersburg
Q5 Britain, France and the Ottoman Empire
Q6 Sergei Witte
Q7 1991
Q8 Ivan the Terrible
Q9 14th century
Q10 Onion

Russia 2 (average)

Q1 Romanov
Q2 1905
Q3 Union of Soviet Socialist Republics
Q4 Michael I
Q5 Alexander Kerensky and Vladimir Ilyich Ulyanov (Lenin)
Q6 Tsarskoe Selo
Q7 Pokrovskoye
Q8 Boris Yeltsin
Q9 The State Duma
Q10 Boris Godunov

Russia 3 (expert)

Q1 Ipatiev House
Q2 1861
Q3 Minister of the Interior

Q4 Russo-Japanese War

Q5 15

Q6 AK-47

Q7 A peasant

Q8 The Golden Horde

Q9 Painting

Q10 Stanislav Petrov

Scandinavia 1 (easy)

Q1 Denmark

Q2 Sweden

Q3 Finland

Q4 Hunter-gatherer

Q5 Temporary dwelling

Q6 Burials

Q7 Kingdom of England

Q8 Battle

Q9 Iceland

Q10 10

Scandinavia 2 (average)

Q1 Olof Palme

Q2 Russia

Q3 Agrarian League

Q4 3

Q5 Sweden

Q6 Harald Bluetooth

Q7 The Kalmar Union

Q8 The Great Northern War

Q9 Erik the Red

Q10 United Kingdom

Scandinavia 3 (expert)

Q1 Tycho Brahe

Q2 Lord High Chancellor of Sweden

Q3 The Viking Age

Q4 5th century

Q5 Olaf Tryggvason

Q6 A female shaman and seer

Q7 1164

Q8 The Winter War

Q9 The Nordic Council

Q10 Vidkun Quisling

Latin America 1 (easy)

Q1 Portugal and the Crown of Castile (Spain)

Q2 Brazil

Q3 John VI

Q4 Peru

Q5 Silver

Q6 Guadalupe Victoria

Q7 Mexican-American War

Q8 3

Q9 Horse riding

Q10 USA

Latin America 2 (average)

Q1 1821

Q2 Pedro I of Brazil

Q3 Latin American wars of independence

Q4 Argentina

Q5 Peruvian War of Independence

Q6 Peru and Bolivia

Q7 Theodore Roosevelt

Q8 Chihuahua

Q9 Napoleon III

Q10 Maya people

Latin America 3 (expert)

Q1 Colombia, Ecuador, Panama, Venezuela, Peru, Guyana, and Brazil
Q2 Buenos Aires
Q3 1824
Q4 The Patria Vieja (1810–1814), the Reconquista (1814–1817), and the Patria Nueva (1817–1823)
Q5 Gran Colombia
Q6 José Manuel Balmaceda
Q7 1890
Q8 Costa Rica, El Salvador, Guatemala, Honduras, and Nicaragua
Q9 Unitarians
Q10 Restorer of the Laws

United Kingdom 1 (easy)

Q1 Suffragettes
Q2 John Bull
Q3 Wales
Q4 Margaret Thatcher
Q5 1973
Q6 Stuart
Q7 Second World War
Q8 25%
Q9 ITV (Independent Television)
Q10 Benjamin Disraeli

United Kingdom 2 (average)

Q1 Sir George Downing
Q2 Blenheim Palace
Q3 England, Scotland and Northern Ireland
Q4 1918-39
Q5 1998
Q6 David Lloyd George
Q7 Economist
Q8 Manchester

Q9 Ireland
Q10 Alfred Hitchcock

<u>United Kingdom 3 (expert)</u>

Q1 14
Q2 HMS *Holland 1*
Q3 Alan Turing
Q4 Emily Davison
Q5 1922
Q6 The *Trent* Affair
Q7 William Gladstone
Q8 Irish Republican Brotherhood
Q9 Henry Mayhew and Ebenezer Landells
Q10 1882

<u>USA 1 (easy)</u>

Q1 Apollo 11
Q2Florida
Q3 13
Q4 Gerald Ford
Q5 San Antonio
Q6 New York
Q7 Woodrow Wilson
Q8 Lyndon Johnson
Q9 Delaware
Q10 4

<u>USA 2 (average)</u>

Q1 1869
Q2 Boston Tea Party
Q3 New Amsterdam
Q4 League of Nations
Q5 Nevada
Q6 George Washington, Thomas Jefferson, Theodore Roosevelt and Abraham Lincoln

Q7 George III
Q8 4
Q9 John Marshall
Q10 The Thirteen Colonies

<u>USA 3 (expert)</u>

Q1 James Monroe
Q2 1845
Q3 Barbary pirates
Q4 Kentucky
Q5 *De oppresso liber*
Q6 Shays' Rebellion
Q7 Bill of Rights
Q8 1940
Q9 Cuba
Q10 Woodstock

<u>Answers: Politics</u>

<u>18th Century Politics 1 (easy)</u>

Q1 Virginia and Maryland
Q2 2
Q3 Prussia
Q4 Catherine the Great
Q5 Slaves
Q6 France and USA
Q7 Peter the Great
Q8 Patrick Henry
Q9 Little Russia
Q10 France

<u>18th Century Politics 2 (average)</u>

Q1 Whig
Q2 William Pitt the Younger
Q3 Christian VII
Q4 Pugachev's Rebellion
Q5 Maria Theresa
Q6 Kingdom of Nepal
Q7 The Society of United Irishmen
Q8 American Revolution and French Revolution
Q9 Peru
Q10 Habsburg

<u>18th Century Politics 3 (expert)</u>

Q1 Sectionalism (the creation of political parties)
Q2 The War of Austrian Succession
Q3 Polish–Lithuanian Commonwealth
Q4 Joseph I
Q5 *Maison Bonaparte*
Q6 1799
Q7 Adam Weishaupt
Q8 Chechens

Q9 1797
Q10 Peshwa of the Maratha Empire

19th Century Politics 1 (easy)

Q1 France
Q2 4
Q3 Ottoman Empire
Q4 Italy
Q5 1
Q6 Abolitionism
Q7 Philippine Revolution
Q8 Francis II, Holy Roman Emperor
Q9 Liberia
Q10 1848

19th Century Politics 2 (average)

Q1 Spencer Perceval
Q2 1833
Q3 Copperheads
Q4 Victor Emmanuel II
Q5 Franco-Prussian War (1870-71)
Q6 Sir Robert Peel
Q7 Urban male working class
Q8 Liberal
Q9 Kingdom of Great Britain and Kingdom of Ireland
Q10 British Empire and Russian Empire

19th Century Politics 3 (expert)

Q1 Alexander Stephens
Q2 Judah Benjamin
Q3 United Kingdom
Q4 Treaty of Amiens
Q5 *Sakoku*
Q6 *Rerum novarum* (Rights and Duties of Capital and Labour)
Q7 Republic of Macedonia

Q8 Kingdom of Hawaii
Q9 Venice
Q10 Dungan Revolt

20th Century Politics 1 (easy)

Q1 Dwight Eisenhower
Q2 Calvin Coolidge
Q3 Clement Atlee
Q4 Europe
Q5 Margaret Thatcher
Q6 The League of Nations
Q7 Cambodia
Q8 Quebec
Q9 Portugal
Q10 William Lyon Mackenzie King

20th Century Politics 2 (average)

Q1 18th Amendment
Q2 Herbert Hoover
Q3 Weimar Republic
Q4 Charles de Gaulle
Q5 Ngo Dinh Diem
Q6 Russia
Q7 African National Congress
Q8 Mohammad Reza Pahlavi (The former Shah of Iran)
Q9 Socialist Party of America
Q10 Geneva, Switzerland

20th Century Politics 3 (expert)

Q1 Wallis Simpson
Q2 Australia
Q3 1948
Q4 Trygve Lie
Q5 Newfoundland
Q6 Cuba

Q7 The former Yugoslav Republic of Macedonia
Q8 1994
Q9 Getúlio Vargas
Q10 Father of the Turks

Also by B.R. Egginton

<u>Non-fiction</u>

Edward VI: England's Boy King

Edward VI's Chronicle (Edward VI)

Richard II: The Tyranny of the White Hart

The Princes in the Tower: An Enigma… 500 Years in the Making

Nicholas II: The Fall of the Romanovs

Henry Hotze: The Master of Confederate Diplomacy

Historiography for Beginners

Archaeology for Beginners

Twelve Olympians: The Greek Pantheon Made Easy

History Essay Writing Basics: For High School and Undergraduate Students

Shorthand SOS: Learn Teeline Shorthand FAST

Public Affairs for Journalists: Concise Edition

Ice Hockey Rulebook

<u>Fiction</u>

The Sixth Number

A Kingdom of Our Own

The Chronicles of Ascension

History Quest: The Plot

The Prince and the Pauper: Annotated Edition (Mark Twain)

<u>Trivia</u>

The Ultimate Mythology Quiz

The Ultimate US Presidents Quiz

The Ultimate British Prime Ministers Quiz

The Ultimate British Royal Navy Quiz

The Ultimate English Monarchs Quiz

The Ultimate French Monarchs Quiz